# 101 VEGETARIAN DISHES
## TRIED-AND-TESTED RECIPES

To: Mary
with all my love
From: your sister
Carol
Christmas 2015

Hylas Publishing
Publisher: Sean Moore
Creative Director: Karen Prince
Designer: Gus Yoo
Editor: Beth Adelman

First Published in 2003 by *BBC Worldwide Ltd*,
Woodlands,

80 Wood Lane, London W12 0TT All photographs © BBC
*Good Food Magazine* 2003 and *BBC Vegetarian Good
Food Magazine* 2003

All the recipes contained in this book first appeared in
*BBC Good Food Magazine* and *BBC Vegetarian Good Food
Magazine*.

Published in the United States by
Hylas Publishing
129 Main Street, Irvington,
New York 10533

Copyright © BBC Worldwide 2002

The moral right of the author has been asserted.

Edited by Gilly Cubitt
Commissioning Editor: Vivien Bowler
Project Editors: Rebecca Hardie and Sarah Miles
Designers: Kathryn Gammon and Annette Peppis
Design Manager: Sarah Ponder
Production Controller: Christopher Tinker

First American Edition published in 2003
02 03 04 05 10 9 8 7 6 5 4 3 2 1

ISBN 1-59258-022-X

Set in Helvetica and ITC Officina Sans

Printed and bound in Italy by LEGO SpA

Color origination by Radstock Reproductions Ltd,
Midsomer Norton

Distributed by St. Martin's Press

# 101 VEGETARIAN DISHES
## TRIED-AND-TESTED RECIPES

Editor-in-chief
**Orlando Murrin**

# Contents

Introduction    6

Soups, Salads & Snacks    10

Light Meals    48

Pasta, Rice & Noodles    86

Main Courses    124

Dairy-free Dishes    156

Desserts    188

Index    212

# Introduction

Conjuring up vegetarian dishes, whether you're a lifelong devotee or someone who wants a change for one night, is not as simple as just leaving out the meat. As vegetarians know, there's much more to veggie cooking than a cheese omelette and a mushroom risotto.

That's why we've picked our all-time favorite recipes from *BBC Good Food Magazine* for this compact but comprehensive book. It's got all those simple but delectable vegetarian recipes you always wish you had up your sleeve. We think you'll find it invaluable whatever the occasion, with ideas for light snacks, main dishes and desserts, plus the trickiest dishes of all—dairy-free.

All the recipes have been tested in the *Good Food* kitchen, guaranteeing you success every time. They're also well balanced and come with a nutritional breakdown, so you can keep track of the calorie, fat and salt content.

As always, our recipes make the most of vegetables in season, plus good use of frozen vegetables and things you are likely to have in your pantry—which count towards your five-a-day recommended servings of fruit and vegetables. So not only will you wow family and friends with fabulous food, like the Spicy Nasi Goreng pictured opposite (see page 116 for recipe), but they'll be getting healthy, balanced meals in the bargain.

Editor, BBC Good Food Magazine

Orlando Murrin

# Conversion tables

NOTES ON THE RECIPES
- Eggs are large, unless stated otherwise.
- Wash all fresh produce before preparation.

## OVEN TEMPERATURES

| °F | °C | Gas | Fan °C | Oven temp. |
|---|---|---|---|---|
| 225 | 110 | ¼ | 90 | Very cool |
| 250 | 120 | ½ | 100 | Very cool |
| 275 | 140 | 1 | 120 | Cool or slow |
| 300 | 150 | 2 | 130 | Cool or slow |
| 325 | 160 | 3 | 140 | Warm |
| 350 | 180 | 4 | 160 | Moderate |
| 375 | 190 | 5 | 170 | Moderately hot |
| 400 | 200 | 6 | 180 | Fairly hot |
| 425 | 220 | 7 | 200 | Hot |
| 450 | 230 | 8 | 210 | Very hot |
| 475 | 240 | 9 | 220 | Very hot |

APPROXIMATE WEIGHT CONVERSIONS
- All the recipes in this book use American measurements. The charts on this page and the next will help you convert to metric measurements. Conversions are approximate and have been rounded up or down. Follow one set of measurements only; do not mix the two.
- Cup measurements have not been listed here, because they vary from ingredient to ingredient. Please use a kitchen scale to weigh dry/solid ingredients.
- Where a recipe calls for a can of something (for example, tuna or tomatoes), we have listed what is generally a standard size can. If the standard cans in your area are a slightly different size, a small difference should not affect the outcome of the recipe.

## SPOON MEASURES

- Spoon measurements are level unless otherwise specified.
- 1 teaspoon = 5ml
- 1 tablespoon = 15ml
- 1 Australian tablespoon = 20ml (cooks in Australia should measure 3 teaspoons where 1 tablespoon is specified in a recipe)

## APPROXIMATE LIQUID CONVERSIONS

| US | Metric | Imperial | Australia |
|---|---|---|---|
| ¼ cup | 50ml | 2fl oz | ¼ cup |
| ½ cup | 125ml | 4fl oz | ½ cup |
| ¾ cup | 175ml | 6fl oz | ¾ cup |
| 1 cup | 225ml | 8fl oz | 1 cup |
| 1¼ cups | 300ml | 10fl oz/½ pint | ½ pint |
| 2 cups/1 pint | 450ml | 16fl oz | 2 cups |
| 2½ cups | 600ml | 20fl oz/1 pint | 1 pint |
| 1 quart | 1 litre | 35fl oz/1¾ pints | 1¾ pints |

A velvety smooth soup with a dramatic
color but gentle flavor.

# Spinach, Sage and Potato Soup

2oz butter
2 red onions, chopped
3 garlic cloves, crushed
1tbsp shredded fresh sage,
plus extra to garnish
2 large potatoes (about
1lb 2oz total), diced
5 cups vegetable stock
9oz baby spinach leaves
salt & pepper to taste
4 tbsp heavy cream,
to serve (optional)

Takes 40 minutes • Serves 4

1 Melt the butter in a large pot and fry the onions
for 5–6 minutes over low heat until slightly softened.
Add the garlic, sage and potatoes, cover and cook
over very low heat for 10 minutes.
2 Stir in the stock, bring to a boil and cook for 5
minutes. Add the spinach and cook for 2 minutes.
Transfer the mixture to a food processor or blender
and process until smooth (you may need to do this in
batches).
3 Return to the pot and heat gently until warmed.
Season to taste with salt and pepper, and serve with
a spoonful of cream, if using, garnished with the
extra sage.

• Per serving: 265 calories, protein 7g, carbohydrate 28g, fat
14g, saturated fat 9g, fiber 4g, added sugar none, salt 1.67g

Celeriac is also known as celery root. Choose the smoothest, least knobby celeriac you can find.

## Celeriac and Blue Cheese Soup

1oz butter
1 medium onion, chopped
1lb 10oz celeriac, peeled and cut into ¾in chunks
1 large baking potato, chopped
2 tbsp chopped fresh sage leaves
2 cups vegetable stock
1 cup cream
8oz blue cheese, diced
salt & pepper to taste
fresh chives and deep-fried sage leaves, to garnish (optional)

Takes 35 minutes • Serves 4

1  Melt the butter in a large pot and gently cook the vegetables and sage for 5 minutes. Stir in the stock and bring to a boil. Cover and simmer for 15 minutes, until the vegetables are tender.
2  Transfer to a food processor and process until smooth (you may need to do this in batches). Return the soup to the pot and stir in the cream and half the blue cheese. Cook over low heat until the cheese has melted, but do not allow to boil. Season to taste with salt and pepper.
3  Divide the soup among four serving bowls and sprinkle with the remaining blue cheese, the chives and deep-fried sage leaves,  to serve.

• Per serving: 488 calories, protein 17g, carbohydrate 27g, fat 35g, saturated fat 22g, fiber 9g, added sugar none, salt 2.78g

The rice will continue to absorb the stock after the soup is cooked.
So if you reheat the soup, you may need to add more stock.

# Baby Spinach and Rice Soup

1 tbsp olive oil
1 onion, chopped
2 garlic cloves, crushed
4oz arborio rice
finely grated zest and juice
of 1 lemon
5 cups vegetable stock
2 large, firm tomatoes, seeded
and chopped
8oz baby spinach leaves, shredded
4oz your favorite vegetarian
pesto sauce
parmesan cheese shavings,
to garnish

Takes 35 minutes • Serves 4

1 Heat the oil in a large pan and saute the onion and garlic for 3–4 minutes until softened. Stir in the rice and cook for 1 minute, stirring occasionally.
2 Add the lemon zest, juice and stock. Bring to a boil and simmer for 15 minutes.
3 Stir the tomatoes, spinach and pesto into the soup. Bring to a boil and simmer for 4–5 minutes, until the rice is tender. Season with salt and pepper and serve sprinkled with the parmesan shavings.

• Per serving: 409 calories, protein 12g, carbohydrate 33g, fat 26g, saturated fat 5g, fiber 3g, added sugar none, salt 1.93g

If you can't buy fresh lemongrass, many supermarkets stock it dried or in jars. Substitute a teaspoon of this instead.

# Hot and Sour Corn Soup

1 corn on the cob
1 tbsp vegetable oil
1 red chili, seeded and sliced
1 shallot, finely chopped
2 stalks lemongrass, bruised
3 baby leeks or scallions, sliced
1 red pepper, seeded and thinly sliced
15oz coconut milk
3 cups pints vegetable stock
2 kaffir lime leaves (optional)
6oz vermicelli egg noodles
juice of 1 lime
salt to taste
small bunch cilantro (coriander), roughly chopped

Takes 35 minutes • Serves 4

1  Hold the corn cob upright on a board, and, using a sharp knife, slice downward to strip the corn kernels from the cob. Heat the oil in a large pot, add the kernels, chili, shallot, lemongrass, leeks or scallions and red pepper, and cook for 3–4 minutes, stirring occasionally.

2  Add the coconut milk, stock and lime leaves, if using. Bring to a boil, then cover. Reduce the heat and simmer gently for 15 minutes. Discard the lemongrass stalks. Add the noodles and cook 4 minutes until tender.

3  Remove from the heat and stir in the lime juice and cilantro. Season with salt, if necessary, and serve immediately.

• Per serving: 545 calories, protein 11g, carbohydrate 41g, fat 39g, saturated fat 27g, fiber 9g, added sugar none, salt 0.97g

Saffron lends a splash of sunny color and flavor to
a simple leek soup, topped with crispy leek rings.

# Saffron and Leek Soup

4 medium leeks
2oz butter
1 tbsp olive oil
good pinch of saffron strands
2 tbsp all-purpose flour
4 cups vegetable stock
salt & pepper to taste
oil, for shallow frying
1 tbsp cornstarch
1 egg white, lightly beaten
2 scallions, sliced on the diagonal

Takes 35 minutes • Serves 4

1 Slice a 3-inch length of leek crosswise. Separate
into rings and set aside. Chop the remaining leeks.
Heat the butter and oil in a large pot and cook the
leeks for 1 minute, stirring. Mix in the saffron and
flour, then gradually stir in the stock, bring to a boil
and simmer gently for 10 minutes, until thickened,
stirring frequently.
2 Transfer the soup to a food processor and
process until smooth. You may need to do this in
batches. Place in a clean pot and season with salt
and pepper. Heat through gently.
3 Meanwhile, heat a little oil in a frying pan. Toss
the leek rings in the cornstarch. Shake off the
excess, then dip the rings into the egg white. Fry the
leek rings until crisp and golden. Drain and serve
scattered over the soup, along with the scallion.

• Per serving: 219 calories, protein 4g, carbohydrate 12g, fat
17g, saturated fat 7g, fiber 2g, added sugar none, salt 1.34g

The flavors of tomatoes and white wine work
really well with celery in this warm salad.

# Celery and White Bean Salad

2oz butter
1½ heads of celery, separated into
stalks and sliced diagonally
1 tbsp chopped fresh rosemary
½ cup dry white wine
½ cup vegetable stock
pinch of saffron strands
1lb tomatoes, skinned, seeded
and cut into wedges
finely grated zest and juice
of ½ lemon
15oz can cannellini or navy beans,
drained and rinsed
2oz pitted black olives
salt & pepper to taste
handful of flatleaf parsley,
roughly torn
crusty bread, to serve

Takes 40 minutes • Serves 4

1  Melt the butter in a large pot and add the
celery and rosemary. Cover and cook gently for 10
minutes, until soft but not browned.
2  Stir in the wine, stock and saffron. Bring to a boil
and boil for 8–10 minutes, until the liquid has
reduced by half.
3  Stir in the tomatoes, lemon zest and juice, and
beans. Bring to a boil and simmer for 5 minutes. Stir
in the olives and season with salt and pepper. Allow
to cool slightly. Scatter the parsley on top and serve
with crusty bread to mop up the juices.

• Per serving: 262 calories, protein 9g, carbohydrate 23g, fat
13g, saturated fat 7g, fiber 9g, added sugar none, salt 2.32g

Tangy kumquats contrast with the earthy
flavors of the mushrooms and sweet red onion.

# Hot Mushroom and Kumquat Salad

5 tbsp olive oil
9oz mixed mushrooms, sliced
1 red onion, sliced
2oz kumquats, sliced
pinch of dried chili flakes
2oz sliced white bread, crusts
removed and cubed
salt & pepper to taste
3oz arugula
1 tbsp white wine vinegar

Takes 30 minutes • Serves 2
(easily doubled)

1  Melt 1 tablespoon of the oil in a frying pan and
saute the mushrooms for 2–3 minutes. Add the
onion and kumquats and cook 2–3 minutes more.
Set aside and keep warm.
2  Mix together the chili flakes, bread cubes and 1
tablespoon of the oil. Season well with salt and
pepper. Heat 1 tablespoon of oil in the frying pan
and fry the bread mixture until crisp and golden.
Divide the arugula among two serving plates and top
with the mushroom and kumquat mix and the chili
croutons.
3  Whisk together the last of the oil with the
vinegar, season, and drizzle over the salad. Serve
immediately.

• Per serving: 488 calories, protein 6g, carbohydrate 19g, fat
39g, saturated fat 6g, fiber 4g, added sugar none, salt 0.46g

Use less salty Lancashire cheese in
place of feta, if you prefer.

# Two Cheese Salad with Croutons

2 thick slices white bread,
crusts removed
1 tsp paprika
2 tbsp olive oil
1 garlic clove, crushed
1 large romaine lettuce
2 ripe avocados
2 tbsp lemon juice
black pepper
1 large zucchini, cut into sticks
5oz feta cheese, crumbled
into chunks
1oz finely grated parmesan cheese
6 tbsp your favorite salad dressing

1 Preheat the oven to 425°F. Cut the bread into
¾-inch cubes. Toss with the paprika, olive oil and
garlic, then spread out on a baking sheet. Bake for
7–8 minutes, until crisp.
2 Tear the lettuce into large pieces. Peel and slice
the avocados and toss with lemon juice and freshly
ground black pepper.
3 Mix the lettuce, zucchini, cheese and croutons.
Put into a large salad bowl with the avocado, and
sprinkle with parmesan. Drizzle dressing over the
salad to serve.

• Per serving: 453 calories, protein 12g, carbohydrate 12g, fat
40g, saturated fat 10g, fiber 4g, added sugar none, salt 1.92g

Takes 30 minutes • Serves 4

A fresh-tasting salad made from summer
vegetables, crumbly cheese and mint.

# English Garden Salad

1lb 2oz new potatoes, sliced thickly
12oz green beans, sliced
bunch of scallions, chopped
6oz sundried tomatoes packed in oil,
drained
8oz Cheshire or Lancashire cheese
good handful of fresh mint leaves,
roughly chopped
4–5 tbsp honey-mustard dressing

Takes 30 minutes • Serves 4

1 Cook the potatoes in salted boiling water for 10 minutes. Add the beans to the pot and cook for a further 4–6 minutes, until the potatoes and beans are just tender.

2 Drain the vegetables and rinse under cold running water. Shake the colander to get rid of as much water as possible, then put into a large bowl. Add the onions and tomatoes, crumble in the cheese and mix well.

3 Add most of the mint and dressing and toss everything lightly together. Place on a serving dish, drizzle with a little more dressing and scatter the rest of the mint on top.

• Per serving: 427 calories, protein 18g, carbohydrate 29g, fat 27g, saturated fat 11g, fiber 6g, added sugar none, salt 2.39g

Check the supermarket for jars of marinated feta cheese in oil.
Use the oil for the dressing.

# Feta and Charred Peach Salad

juice of 1 lime
4 fresh ripe peaches, each cut
into wedges
6oz mixed salad greens
10oz marinated feta cheese in oil
1 red onion, sliced
2 tbsp chopped fresh mint
salt & pepper to taste

Takes 10 minutes • Serves 4

1 Heat a lightly greased griddle pan until it's very hot. Squeeze the lime juice over the peaches and place them on the griddle pan. Cook them for 2–3 minutes, turning, until nicely charred.
2 In a large salad bowl, mix together the salad greens, feta, 2 tablespoons of the oil from the feta, the red onion and chopped mint. Season well with salt and pepper.
3 Divide among four plates and top with the charred peaches. Sprinkle with black pepper and serve.

• Per serving: 272 calories, protein 11g, carbohydrate 11g, fat 21g, saturated fat 9g, fiber 2g, added sugar none, salt 2.32g

Choose a small, soft goat cheese. The rind is edible,
but discard the ends to make four matching slices.

# Goat Cheese Salad

4oz soft goat cheese
1 oval roll, cut into 4 slices
and ends discarded
salt & pepper to taste
4 tsp olive oil
1 tsp lemon juice or white
wine vinegar
½ tsp wholegrain or Dijon mustard
1 garlic clove, chopped
handful of mixed salad greens

Takes 10 minutes • Serves 1
(easily multiplied)

1  Preheat the broiler. Cut the cheese into four
slices. Toast the bread slices on both sides, then top
with the cheese.
2  Sprinkle with black pepper and a little of the olive
oil and broil for 2–3 minutes.
3  Meanwhile, mix together the remaining olive oil,
lemon juice or vinegar, mustard and garlic. Season
with salt and pepper, then toss with the salad leaves.
Pile on to a plate and top with the cheese toasts.

• Per serving: 509 calories, protein 19g, carbohydrate 16g, fat
42g, saturated fat 15g, fiber 1g, added sugar none, salt 1.84g

Use real Greek feta for the best flavor. A package keeps for about six months unopened in the refrigerator, so it's a great supper standby.

# Feta and White Bean Salad

4oz baby spinach leaves
10oz large tomatoes, cut into wedges
15oz can navy or cannellini beans, drained and rinsed
1 small red onion, finely chopped
6oz feta cheese
crusty bread, to serve

FOR THE DRESSING
1 garlic clove, finely chopped
1 tbsp lemon juice
1 tsp honey
3 tbsp olive oil
salt & pepper to taste

Takes 10–20 minutes • Serves 4

1 Cover a large platter or shallow dish with the spinach leaves. Scatter the tomato wedges over the spinach, followed by the beans and red onion.
2 Drain off the liquid from the feta and crumble the cheese over the vegetables.
3 Place the dressing ingredients in a small bowl, season with salt and pepper, and whisk with a fork until slightly thickened. Drizzle over the salad, and serve with crusty bread.

• Per serving: 515 calories, protein 31g, carbohydrate 56g, fat 20g, saturated fat 8g, fiber 19g, added sugar 1g, salt 2.05g

The traditional combination of tomatoes, olives and feta cheese
is made more substantial by adding pasta.

# Greek Pasta Salad

10oz fusilli (spirals) or farfalle
(bowties) or penne (tubes)
7oz fresh baby spinach leaves
8oz cherry tomatoes, halved
4oz kalamata olives
8oz feta cheese, broken into
rough chunks
black pepper
3 tbsp olive oil
crusty bread, to serve

Takes 30 minutes • Serves 4

1  Cook the pasta in a large pot of salted boiling water for 10 minutes. Throw in the spinach, stir well and boil for another 2 minutes. Drain into a colander and leave to drip dry.

2  Put the tomatoes, olives and feta in a large bowl, grind lots of black pepper over, and then drizzle with the olive oil.

3  Toss in the drained pasta and spinach, and serve with crusty bread.

• Per serving: 418 calories, protein 18g, carbohydrate 37g, fat 23g, saturated fat 8g, fiber 5g, added sugar 0.1g, salt 3.48g

Tzatziki is Greek yogurt and cucumber salad,
usually eaten as a dip for pita bread.

# Beet and Tzatziki Sandwich

knob of softened butter
2 thick slices 12-grain bread
3 tbsp plain, mild yogurt
1½in piece cucumber, grated
and drained
2 tbsp chopped fresh mint, plus
extra leaves to garnish
salt & pepper to taste
handful of mixed salad green
1 small cooked beet, sliced

Takes 10 minutes • Serves 1
(easily multiplied)

1  Spread the softened butter on one side of each slice of bread.

2  To make the tzatziki, mix together the yogurt, grated cucumber and chopped mint in a small bowl. Season well with salt and pepper.

3  Place a handful of mixed salad greens on each slice of bread. Arrange the beet slices on top of the salad leaves and spoon over the tzatziki. Sprinkle with the extra mint leaves.

• Per serving: 433 calories, protein 13g, carbohydrate 60g, fat 18g, saturated fat 11g, fiber 2g, added sugar none, salt 1.63g

English muffins make instant pizza crusts. Use pesto
instead of tomato sauce, if you have some handy.

# Mini Muffin Pizzas

1 very small zucchini
1 english muffin
2 tbsp tomato sauce
2 sundried tomatoes, thinly sliced
1½oz mozzarella cheese, cubed
1 tsp torn fresh oregano leaves
black pepper
2 tsp olive oil

Takes 15 minutes • Serves 1
(easily multiplied)

1 Preheat the broiler. Using a potato peeler, shred
the zucchini lengthwise into thin ribbons.
2 Split the muffin in half. Spread the cut halves with
the sauce and toast for 1–2 minute,s until hot.
3 Arrange the zucchini over the muffin halves. Top
with the sundried tomatoes, cheese and oregano.
Season with black pepper. Drizzle with the olive oil
and broil for 2 minutes.

• Per serving: 448 calories, protein 15g, carbohydrate 39g, fat
27g, saturated fat 9g, fiber 3g, added sugar 1g, salt 1.81g

Broil the smoked cheese until just golden and eat it
immediately, because it becomes chewy when it cools.

# Smoked Cheese and Tomato Pita

2 romaine lettuce leaves, shredded
1 plum tomato, sliced
1 thin slice sweet onion, separated
into rings
1 sprig fresh mint, chopped
1 tsp olive oil
salt & pepper to taste
3 thick slices smoked cheese (such
as gouda, cheddar or edam)
1 pita bread

Takes 10 minutes • Serves 1
(easily multiplied)

1  Preheat the broiler. Put the lettuce, tomato slices,
onion rings and mint in a bowl, toss with the olive oil
and season with salt and pepper.
2  Place the cheese slices on a baking sheet and
broil for about 2 minutes until they are turning
golden.
3  Broil the pita pocket for a few seconds on each
side until it puffs open. Tuck the cheese and salad
inside the pita and eat immediately.

• Per serving: 375 calories, protein 16g, carbohydrate 46g, fat
15g, saturated fat 7g, fiber 3g, added sugar none, salt 1.45g

Turn ordinary sliced white bread into garlicky
crispbreads for these warm sandwiches.

# Ricotta-stuffed Crispbreads

8 slices white bread, crusts removed
2oz garlic butter, melted
3 tbsp olive oil
1 red and 1 yellow pepper, halved,
seeded and chopped
8oz savoy cabbage, torn
8oz cherry tomatoes, halved
1 tbsp white wine vinegar
salt & pepper to taste
8oz ricotta cheese
handful of basil, plus fresh basil
leaves, to serve

Takes 20 minutes • Serves 4

1  Preheat the oven to 400°F. Roll out each slice of
bread with a rolling pin until flattened. Place on
baking sheets and brush with the garlic butter. Bake
for 10 minutes until crisp.
2  Heat 2 tablespoons of the oil in a pan, add the
peppers and cook until lightly charred. Add the
cabbage and cook for 2–3 minutes. Remove from
the heat, add the tomatoes and vinegar and season
with salt and pepper.
3  Mix the ricotta cheese and basil. Spread four of
the bread slices with the ricotta mixture. Top with the
vegetables and place another slice of bread on top.
Drizzle with the remaining olive oil and garnish with
the fresh basil.

• Per serving: 385 calories, protein 10g, carbohydrate 21g, fat
30g, saturated fat 13g, fiber 4g, added sugar 0.2g, salt 0.7g

Ciabatta (the word means "slipper") is a small Italian bread that's crusty on the outside and light on the inside.

# Broccoli and Poached Egg Toasts

8oz broccoli, cut into thin florets
1 ciabatta loaf
1 garlic clove, halved
2 tbsp olive oil
1 tbsp Dijon mustard
6 shallots, halved lengthwise
4 eggs
salt & pepper to taste

Takes 25 minutes • Serves 4

1  Blanch the broccoli in boiling water for 1 minute. Drain and refresh in cold water. Dry on paper towels. Heat a griddle or frying pan.

2  Cut the ciabatta in half lengthwise, then cut each slice in half. Rub with the garlic and brush with half the oil. Cook the ciabatta on the griddle for 1–2 minutes on each side until golden. Spread with the mustard and keep warm. Toss the shallots in the remaining olive oil and cook cut-side down on the griddle for 2 minutes on each side. Keep warm.

3  Pile the broccoli on to the griddle and cook for 3–4 minutes, turning frequently. Meanwhile, poach the eggs in gently simmering water until set to your liking. Pile the shallots and broccoli on the ciabatta. Top with the eggs and season with salt and pepper.

• Per serving: 380 calories, protein 17g, carbohydrate 47g, fat 15g, saturated fat 3g, fiber 4g, added sugar none, salt 1.49g

You should be able to find all these ingredients at the deli counter. Buy some good bread to go with it.

## Olive and Ricotta Pâté

1lb ricotta cheese
2oz parmesan cheese, finely grated
2 medium egg whites, lightly beaten
salt & pepper to taste
7oz marinated green olives
6oz can pitted black olives, drained
4 sundried tomatoes, roughly chopped
2 sprigs fresh rosemary, leaves only
bread and roasted tomatoes, to serve

Takes 40 minutes • Serves 6

1  Preheat the oven to 400°F. Line an 8-inch square baking pan with oiled baking parchment. In a large bowl, beat together the ricotta, parmesan and egg whites, and season with salt and pepper.
2  Spoon into the prepared cake tin and level the surface with the back of a wet spoon. Press the olives, sundried tomatoes and rosemary into the surface and bake for 25–30 minutes, until firm.
3  Turn out and remove the paper. Serve in wedges with bread and roasted tomatoes.

• Per serving: 227 calories, protein 12g, carbohydrate 3g, fat 19g, saturated fat 8g, fiber 2g, added sugar none, salt 4.07g

This is a wonderfully creamy mixture, yet the
fresh flavors of the vegetables still shine through.

# Minted Spring Vegetables

1oz butter
1 tbsp olive oil
8oz baby onions
7fl oz dry white wine
2 medium leeks, halved and cut
into 2in ribbons
12oz frozen baby peas
2 small heads of Boston lettuce,
quartered lengthwise
7fl oz crème fraîche (or cream
mixed with 1/2 tsp buttermilk)
2 tbsp chopped fresh mint
2 tbsp chopped fresh flatleaf parsley
salt & pepper to taste
bulghar wheat or couscous, to serve

Takes 35 minutes • Serves 4

1 Heat the butter and olive oil in a large non-stick frying pan until lightly foaming. Add the baby onions and cook over low heat for 8 minutes. Add the wine and leeks and bring to a boil. Simmer for 5 minutes, until the leeks are tender.

2 Add the peas and simmer 5 minutes more. Add the lettuce and simmer another 3 minutes.

3 Stir in the crème fraîche and herbs. Season well with salt and pepper and warm through very gently for 2–3 minutes. Serve spooned over hot bulghar wheat or couscous.

• Per serving: 321 calories, protein 9g, carbohydrate 18g, fat 20g, saturated fat 10g, fiber 8g, added sugar none, salt 0.23g

Sounds strange, but take the pan off the heat before you add the salad ingredients and you'll love the fresh-tasting result.

# Stir-fried Salad with Almonds

3 tbsp olive oil
3oz whole blanched almonds
1 bunch scallions, sliced
1 small cucumber, peeled, seeded and sliced
3 stalks celery, cut crosswise
8oz small tomatoes, quartered
1 small Boston lettuces, torn in pieces
1oz watercress
25g/1oz fresh cilantro (coriander)
juice of ½ lemon
½ tsp sugar
salt & pepper to taste
crusty bread or rice, to serve

Takes 15 minutes • Serves 4

1  Heat 2 tablespoons of the oil in a frying pan or wok and fry the almonds for 2–3 minutes until golden. Drain on paper towels, then chop roughly.
2  Add the remaining oil to the pan and, when hot, add the scallions, cucumber, celery and tomatoes and stir fry for 2 minutes. Remove from the heat, add the remaining ingredients and toss until combined. Season with salt and pepper.
3  Spoon the warm salad on to serving plates and scatter the almonds on top. Spoon the pan juices over the dish and serve with crusty bread or rice.

• Per serving: 247 calories, protein 6g, carbohydrate 6g, fat 22g, saturated fat 2g, fiber 3g, added sugar 1g, salt 0.09g

Blinis make perfect bases for canapés and starters.
Try them with herb cream cheese, tomatoes and arugula.

# Vegetable Blini Stacks

8oz asparagus spears, trimmed
4oz sugarsnap peas
5oz broccoli florets
8oz crème fraîche (or creams mixed with 1/2 tsp buttermilk)
1½ tbsp fresh pesto
handful of fresh basil, roughly torn
salt & pepper to taste
8 large, ready-made blinis (about 4in diameter)
5oz sundried tomatoes packed in oil, drained

Takes 20 minutes • Serves 4

1  Preheat the oven to 350°F. Bring a large pot of salted water to a boil. Add the asparagus, sugarsnap peas and broccoli and cook for 2 minutes until just tender. Drain and set aside. Combine the crème fraîche, pesto and half the basil. Season with salt and pepper.
2  Place four blinis on a large baking dish. Top with the vegetables and tomatoes and spoon on the crème fraîche mixture.
3  Halve the remaining blinis and place on top of the vegetables. Bake for 8 minutes until heated through.

• Per serving: 372 calories, protein 10g, carbohydrate 20g, fat 28g, saturated fat 13g, fiber 4g, added sugar none, salt 0.43g

It sounds exotic, but frozen stir fry vegetables plus coconut
add up to a tasty but easy Thai-style meal.

# Thai Coconut Vegetable Soup

1 tbsp vegetable oil
1oz fresh ginger, peeled
and sliced
2 garlic cloves, sliced
2 lemongrass stalks, bruised
3–4 bird's eye chilies, bruised
4 kaffir lime leaves, bruised
15oz can coconut milk
7oz coconut cream
1lb 2oz mixed stir fry vegetables
fresh basil and cilantro (coriander)
leaves, to garnish

Takes 30 minutes • Serves 3

1  Heat the oil in a frying pan or wok and
stir fry the ginger, garlic, lemongrass and chilies for
30 seconds.
2  Add the lime leaves to the pan and pour in
coconut milk and cream. Bring to a boil, cover and
simmer gently for about 15 minutes, stirring
occasionally.
3  Add the vegetables and return to a boil. Simmer
for 2–3 minutes, stirring frequently, until the
vegetables are just tender. Ladle into bowls and
garnish with the fresh basil and cilantro.

• Per serving: 917 calories, protein 11g, carbohydrate 20g, fat
80g, saturated fat 72g, fiber 18g, added sugar 1g, salt 0.18g

Curry can be deceivingly high in fat. This version is packed
with flavor and has only 5g of fat per serving.

# Spicy Vegetable Chapati Wraps

10oz sweet potatoes, peeled
and roughly cubed
15oz can peeled plum tomatoes
15oz can chickpeas, drained
½ tsp dried chili flakes
2 tbsp mild curry paste
4oz baby spinach leaves
2 tbsp chopped fresh cilantro
(coriander)
4 plain chapatis (Indian flatbreads)
4 tbsp fat-free mild yogurt

Takes 25 minutes • Serves 4

1 Cook the sweet potatoes in salted boiling water
for 10–12 minutes, until tender. Meanwhile, put the
tomatoes, chickpeas, chili flakes and curry paste in
another pan and simmer gently for about 5 minutes,
stirring all the time.

2 Preheat the broiler. Drain the sweet potatoes and
add to the tomato mixture. Stir in the spinach and
cook for a minute, until just starting to wilt. Stir in
the cilantro, season to taste and keep warm.

3 Sprinkle the chapatis with a little water and broil
for 20–30 seconds each side. Spoon on the filling,
top with yogurt and fold in half to serve.

• Per serving: 289 calories, protein 12g, carbohydrate 54g, fat
5g, saturated fat none, fiber 5g, added sugar none, salt 1.08g

A simple potato cake makes a welcome change
from toast with your fried egg.

## Rösti with Egg and Onions

4 tsp olive oil
½ red or white onion, finely sliced
2oz potato, coarsely grated
1 tsp wholegrain mustard
salt & pepper to taste
1 medium egg
2 tomatoes, sliced
drizzle of balsamic vinegar

Takes 15 minutes • Serves 1
(easily multiplied)

1  Heat half the oil in a non-stick frying pan. Fry half the onion until crispy. Drain and reserve. Mix the potato with the rest of the onion, mustard and seasoning.

2  Add the remaining oil to the pan, then add the potato mixture and press into a 4½-inch round. Fry for 8–10 minutes until golden, turning several times. Fry the egg alongside the rösti.

3  Arrange the tomatoes on a plate and drizzle with the balsamic vinegar. Serve the rösti on the tomatoes with the egg and crispy onion on top.

• Per serving: 335 calories, protein 9g, carbohydrate 16g, fat 27g, saturated fat 4g, fiber 3g, added sugar none, salt 0.53g

Tapenade is a thick purée of olives, capers,
garlic and olive oil (but watch out for hidden anchovies).

# Soufflé Avocado Omelette

3 medium eggs, separated
1 tbsp milk
2 tbsp chopped fresh flatleaf parsley
salt & pepper to taste
2 tsp olive oil
2 tbsp black olive tapenade
1 small avocado, halved,
pitted and sliced
juice of ½ lemon
tomato salad, to serve (optional)

Takes 10 minutes • Serves 4

1  Place the egg whites in a large bowl and whisk to
soft peaks. Place the egg yolks in a separate bowl
with the milk and parsley. Season with salt and
pepper and beat together. Add a quarter of the
whites to the yolks and gently stir. Fold in the
remaining egg whites.
2  Preheat the broiler. Heat the oil in an 8-inch
non-stick frying pan. Add the egg mixture and cook
for 2–3 minutes, until lightly set. Place under the
broiler for 1–2 minutes to cook the top.
3  Spoon the olive tapenade over one half
of the omelette. Top with the avocado and squeeze
on the lemon juice. Fold over the other half, transfer
to a plate and serve with a tomato salad, if you like.

• Per serving: 717 calories, protein 21g, carbohydrate 21g, fat
70g, saturated fat 12g, fiber 4g, added sugar none, salt 2.39g

As the name suggests, there's no pastry;
just chunky vegetables set in eggs.

# Crustless Vegetable Quiche

1 tbsp vegetable oil
1 yellow and 1 orange pepper, cut
into quarters and seeded
2 zucchini, cut into chunks
2 large red onions, cut into wedges
4 medium eggs, beaten
3½fl oz milk
2 tbsp fresh pesto
salt & pepper to taste
green salad, to serve

Takes 40 minutes • Serves 4

1  Preheat the oven to 200°C. Heat the oil in a wok or large frying pan and stir fry the peppers, zucchini and onions over high heat for 2–3 minutes.
2  Transfer the vegetables to an oiled 2-quart ovenproof dish. In a large bowl, mix together the eggs, milk, pesto and salt and pepper.
3  Pour over the vegetables and bake for 25 minutes, until firm to the touch in the center. Serve warm with a crisp green salad.

• Per serving: 211 calories, protein 9g, carbohydrate 10g, fat 15g, saturated fat 3g, fiber 2g, added sugar none, salt 0.36g

This quick and easy tart will keep
in the refrigerator up to three days.

# Tomato and Chive Tart

12oz prepared pie crust
7 oz crème fraîche (or cream mixed
with 1/2 tsp buttermilk)
2 eggs
2 tbsp green or red pesto
salt & pepper to taste
6 ripe tomatoes, sliced
8oz cherry tomatoes, halved
snipped fresh chives
green salad, to serve

Takes 35 minutes • Serves 6

1 Preheat the oven to 425°F. Roll out the pastry and use to line the base and sides of a 9 × 13-inch cookie pan.
2 Mix the crème fraîche, eggs and pesto then season with salt and pepper. Pour this creamy mixture over the pastry. Scatter both kinds of tomatoes on top, then season and bake for 20 minutes until set.
3 Toss on some chives and serve cut into big squares, warm or cold, with a green salad.

• Per serving: 426 calories, protein 7g, carbohydrate 31g, fat 31g, saturated fat 13g, fiber 2g, added sugar none, salt 0.58g

This couldn't be simpler. Just arrange the topping
in neat rows on storebought puff pastry.

# Brie and Tomato Tart

9oz puff pastry
8oz brie
4–5 large ripe tomatoes
8oz zucchini
½ tsp dried oregano
salt & pepper to taste

Takes 45 minutes • Serves 4

1  Preheat the oven to 400ºF. Roll out the pastry to a 9 × 12-inch rectangle, put on a damp baking sheet, and score the pastry with a knife 1 inch from the edges all around. Prick the base with a fork, inside the marks.

2  Slice the brie, tomatoes and zucchini into thin slices. Heat 2 tablespoons of olive oil in a frying pan and fry the zucchini for 1–2 minutes until softened. Add the oregano and season with salt and pepper. Cook for 1–2 minutes; cool slightly.

3  Starting from one short end, arrange four overlapping rows of brie, tomatoes and zucchini within the cut marks. Drizzle with the pan juices, and season. Bake for 25–30 minutes, until the pastry is puffed up and the zucchini is tender. Serve warm.

• Per serving: 419 calories, protein 15g, carbohydrate 27g, fat 29g, saturated fat 9g, fiber 2g, added sugar none, salt 1.41g

The big mushrooms cook to a moist firmness under their cloak of peppers and melting goat's cheese.

# Stuffed Mushroom Buschettas

4 thick slices country-style bread, white or brown
2oz softened butter beaten with 1 chopped garlic clove
4 large, flat mushrooms (such as portobellos)
olive oil, for drizzling
salt & pepper to taste
6oz roasted red peppers, either strips in oil or whole peppers in brine
5oz firm goat's cheese
mixed salad, to serve

Takes 40 minutes • Serves 2

1 Preheat the oven to 375°F. Spread both sides of each slice of bread with garlic butter (no need to remove the crusts). Put the bread slices in one layer on a baking sheet.

2 Put a mushroom on top of each slice and drizzle with a little olive oil. Season with salt and pepper. Drain the peppers, slice if necessary, and divide among the mushrooms.

3 Cut the goat's cheese into four slices and put one slice on top of each stack. Bake for 25–30 minutes, until the mushrooms are cooked and the cheese golden. Serve with a mixed salad.

• Per serving: 679 calories, protein 27g, carbohydrate 45g, fat 45g, saturated fat 27g, fiber 5g, added sugar none, salt 2.9g

This dish is perfect for easy entertaining
on nights at home with friends.

# Cheese and Chutney Melts

4 large, crusty rolls
2 tbsp olive oil
salt & pepper to taste
4 tbsp green tomato chutney
4 small goat's cheeses
4 sprigs thyme
green salad, to serve (optional)

Takes 30 minutes • Serves 4

1 Preheat the oven to 375°F. Cut a deep hollow in the top of each roll. Remove the bread from the center and brush the insides with the oil. Season with salt and pepper. Place on a baking sheet and bake for 5 minutes, until lightly crisped.

2 Spoon the chutney into the rolls. Remove the rind from the top and bottom of each cheese and place one in each of the rolls. Push a sprig of thyme into the top and season with black pepper.

3 Scrunch foil around the roll, leaving the cheese uncovered. Bake for 15–20 minutes, until the cheese is golden and bubbling, removing the foil for the last 5 minutes. Serve with a green salad, if you like.

• Per serving: 399 calories, protein 15g, carbohydrate 45g, fat 19g, saturated fat 7g, fiber 1g, added sugar 3g, salt 1.68g

Remember that the mushrooms shrink during cooking.
You could use medium mushrooms and serve more.

# Herb Stuffed Mushrooms

4 very large flat mushrooms
2 tbsp olive oil
salt & pepper to taste

FOR THE STUFFING
3 sprigs fresh thyme
4 tbsp chopped fresh flatleaf parsley
4oz roasted, shelled pistachio
nuts, chopped
3oz pitted black olives, chopped
finely grated zest and juice
of ½ lemon
4oz white breadcrumbs
5oz feta cheese, cut into
small cubes
salt & pepper to taste
crusty bread, to serve
green salad, to serve (optional)

Takes 30 minutes • Serves 4

1  Preheat the oven to 400°F. Remove the mushroom stems and chop roughly. Brush the mushrooms with a little olive oil. Place in a roasting pan and season with salt and pepper. Bake for 10 minutes, until thy are beginning to soften.
2  Meanwhile, mix all the stuffing ingredients with the chopped mushroom stems and the remaining olive oil. Season with salt and pepper.
3  Spoon the stuffing on top of the mushrooms and bake 5–8 minutes more, until the feta begins to soften. Serve immediately on toasted crusty bread with a green salad, if you like.

• Per serving: 433 calories, protein 15g, carbohydrate 24g, fat 31g, saturated fat 8g, fiber 2g, added sugar none, salt 2.96g

Ready-made polenta is sold in large packages that look like a big yellow salami. It's not to be confused with quick-cook polenta.

## Pizza-topped Polenta

16oz ready-made polenta
½ tsp dried oregano
1oz freshly grated parmesan cheese
2oz cheddar cheese, grated
4 tbsp olive oil
4 large, flat mushrooms, stems removed
salt & pepper to taste
14oz ripe tomatoes, roughly chopped
1 garlic clove, finely chopped

Takes 55 minutes • Serves 4

1 Preheat the oven to 425°F. Cut the polenta into 12 slices, ½-inch thick, and lay in four overlapping piles in a roasting pan. Sprinkle with oregano and most of the cheese. Pour the oil in a bowl, season with salt and pepper and brush each mushroom. Place stem-side up on the polenta piles.
2 Add the tomatoes and garlic to the remaining oil. Spoon the tomatoes and their juices in and around the mushrooms and polenta, then season.
3 Sprinkle over the remaining cheese. Roast for 30 minutes until the tomatoes have softened and the mushrooms are tender. Serve hot.

• Per serving: 422 calories, protein 14g, carbohydrate 50g, fat 20g, saturated fat 6g, fiber 3g, added sugar none, salt 0.42g

Smoked cheese can be toasted in a pan without much oil—
softening the cheese rather than melting it.

# Smoked Cheese and Vegetable Fry

3 tbsp olive oil
9oz smoked cheese, cut into slices
2 medium onions, cut in wedges
3 zucchini, sliced
8 tomatoes, halved
16oz can lima beans, drained
salt & pepper to taste

Takes 30 minutes • Serves 4

1 Heat 2 tablespoons of the oil in a roasting pan or large frying pan, add the cheese slices and cook until golden on both sides. Lift out, cut each slice into quarters and set aside. Add the onions to the pan and saute for 5 minutes until golden.

2 Toss in the zucchini and saute until golden. Remove the onions and zucchini from the pan and set aside. Heat the remaining oil in the pan and fry the tomatoes until softened and juicy.

3 Return the onions, zucchini and cheese to the pan, and toss in the beans. Warm through, gently tossing it all together as you go. Season with salt and
pepper and serve.

• Per serving: 285 calories, protein 20g, carbohydrate 29g, fat 22g, saturated fat 9g, fiber 8g, added sugar none, salt 2.35g

Polenta slices are also good cooked on a hot,
oiled griddle, turned once, until pleasantly charred.

# Polenta Dolcelatte Grill

1lb 2oz ready-made polenta,
thickly sliced
2 tbsp olive oil
salt & pepper to taste
3 plum tomatoes, cut into wedges
5oz dolcelatte, cubed
6 tbsp chili jam
green beans, to serve

Takes 45 minutes • Serves 4

1  Preheat the broiler. Place the polenta slices on the broiler pan, brush with olive oil and season well. Broil for 10–15 minutes, until lightly charred. Turn over, brush with oil and broil 10 minutes more.
2  Arrange the polenta and tomato wedges in a shallow, heatproof dish, and drizzle with the remaining olive oil. broil for 5–10 minutes, until the tomatoes soften. Top with the dolcelatte. Broil for 2–3 minutes until melted.
3  Meanwhile, place the chili jam in a small pan and heat gently for 1–2 minutes. Place the grilled polenta, cheese and tomatoes on a plate with a spoonful of the chili jam. Serve with green beans.

• Per serving: 523 calories, protein 16g, carbohydrate 59g, fat 27g, saturated fat 10g, fiber 2g, added sugar none, salt 3.55g

Couscous just needs soaking, so it's the
perfect accompaniment to a speedy pan fry.

# Tofu and Pepper Couscous

5½oz couscous
10oz mixed marinated peppers
2 tbsp olive oil
1 garlic clove, crushed
5oz mixed mushrooms, sliced
5oz firm tofu, cubed
½oz mixed fresh herbs (oregano,
basil, flatleaf parsley), finely
chopped, plus extra, to garnish

Takes 15 minutes • Serves 2

1 Place the couscous in a shallow dish and add 1 cup boiling water. Cover tightly with plastic wrap and leave for 5 minutes. Meanwhile, pour the peppers into a small pan and heat gently for 3–4 minutes.

2 Heat 1 tablespoon of the olive oil in a large frying pan and saute the garlic for 1 minute. Add the mushrooms and saute for 3–4 minutes, until lightly golden. Set aside. Meanwhile, add the remaining olive oil to the pan and cook the tofu for 2 minutes, until lightly golden.

3 Stir the peppers and chopped herbs through the couscous and season. Spoon onto plates and top with the pan-fried tofu and mushrooms. Garnish with the extra herbs and serve.

• Per serving: 695 calories, protein 29g, carbohydrate 48g, fat 44g, saturated fat 17g, fiber 4g, added sugar none, salt 0.94g

A simple but filling supper speeded up
with help from the microwave.

# Cheesy Bread Pudding

1oz butter, softened
6 slices white bread (day-old bread is best)
4 medium eggs, beaten
3½oz milk
2oz parmesan cheese, finely grated
1 tbsp Dijon mustard
1oz cheddar cheese, grated
tomato and scallion salad, to serve

Takes 25 minutes • Serves 4

1  Spread the butter on one side of each slice of bread and cut into triangles. Arrange in a 2-quart microwave-safe dish.
2  In a bowl, mix together the eggs, milk, parmesan and mustard and pour over the bread. Leave to stand for 5 minutes. Preheat the broiler. Microwave the bread mixture on High for 5 minutes.
3  Sprinkle on the cheddar and broil for 2–3 minutes, until golden. Serve hot with a tomato and scallion salad.

• Per serving: 312 calories, protein 17g, carbohydrate 20g, fat 19g, saturated fat 9g, fiber 1g, added sugar none, salt 1.56g

This tart can be stretched to feed extra people,
with a big mixed salad and garlic bread.

# Stilton and Walnut Tart

1lb 5oz onions
1 tbsp balsamic vinegar
salt & pepper to taste
13oz prepared puff pastry
6oz stilton cheese
2oz walnut pieces

Takes 45 minutes • Serves 6

1 Preheat the oven to 400°F. Peel the onions and thinly slice them. Heat 3 tablespoons of olive oil in a large frying pan, add the onions and saute until softened and lightly browned, stirring occasionally. This will take about 10 minutes.

2 Splash in the vinegar, season with salt and pepper, then cook 5 minutes more, until lightly caramelized. Leave to cool while you prepare the pastry. Unroll the pastry and use to line a /9 × 13-inch shallow cookie pan.

3 Spread the onions on the pastry, then crumble the stilton on top and scatter the walnuts. Bake for 15–20 minutes, until the pastry is crisp and golden and the cheese has melted. Cool for 5 minutes before serving, cut into squares.

• Per serving: 446 calories, protein 13g, carbohydrate 31g, fat 31g, saturated fat 7g, fiber 2g, added sugar none, salt 1.19g

This dish is quick and tasty and cooked in one pot,
so there's hardly any washing up.

# Spaghetti Genovese

10oz new potatoes, sliced
10oz spaghetti
8oz trimmed green beans,
cut in half
4oz fresh pesto
salt & pepper to taste
olive oil, for drizzling

Takes 20 minutes • Serves 4

1  Pour boiling water into a very large pot until half full. Return to a boil, then add the potatoes and spaghetti, and a little salt.
2  Cook for 10 minutes until the potatoes and pasta are almost tender. Add the green beans and cook for 5 minutes more.
3  Drain well, reserving 4 tablespoons of the cooking liquid. Return the potatoes, pasta and beans to the pot, then stir in the fresh pesto and reserved cooking liquid. Season with salt and pepper to taste, divide among four serving plates and drizzle with a little olive oil.

• Per serving: 330 calories, protein 23g, carbohydrate 8g, fat 23g, saturated fat 9g, fiber trace, added sugar 7g, salt 0.5g

A simple sauce based on a can of beans from the pantry,
plus wine and cream for richness.

## Pasta with Flageolet Beans

2 tbsp olive oil
2 small red onions, cut into
thick wedges
4 garlic cloves, roughly chopped
15oz can flageolet or navy beans,
drained and rinsed
1 tbsp chopped fresh rosemary
½ cup vegetable stock
½ cup white wine
salt & pepper to taste
4 tbsp heavy cream
4oz green beans
12oz pappardelle (broad
pasta ribbons)

Takes 40 minutes • Serves 4

1  Heat the oil in large pan, add the onions and cook until softened. Add the garlic, beans, rosemary, stock and wine, and simmer for 10 minutes.
2  Season with salt and pepper, add the cream and simmer 5 minutes more. Meanwhile, bring a pot of lightly salted water to a boil. Add the green beans and cook for 5 minutes, until tender. Remove with a slotted spoon and keep hot.
3  Add the pasta to the boiling water and cook according to the package instructions. Drain and toss with the creamy sauce. Divide among four bowls and serve topped with the green beans.

• Per serving: 582 calories, protein 21g, carbohydrate 85g, fat 18g, saturated fat 6g, fiber 9g, added sugar none, salt 0.95g

Egg yolks and cream make one of the quickest
and most delicious pasta sauces.

# Spaghetti Carbonara

12oz tricolor spaghetti
8oz baby carrots, halved lengthwise
thin asparagus, sliced into
1¼in lengths
1 large zucchini, cut into ribbons
2 medium egg yolks
7fl oz heavy cream
2oz parmesan cheese, grated
salt & pepper to taste
2oz sundried tomatoes packed in oil,
drained and sliced

Takes 25 minutes • Serves 4

1  Cook the pasta in a large pot of lightly salted
boiling water according to the package instructions.
About 4 minutes before the end of the cooking time,
add the carrots.
2  After 2 minutes add the asparagus, and just
before draining stir in the zucchini ribbons. Drain
and return to the pan over a low heat. Beat together
the egg yolks, cream and half the parmesan and
season well with salt and pepper.
3  Pour over the pasta and vegetables and heat very
gently for 2–3 minutes, stirring constantly, until the
sauce has thickened slightly (do not overheat or the
eggs will scramble). Stir in the sundried tomatoes
and serve with the remaining parmesan and plenty
of black pepper.

• Per serving: 651 calories, protein 20g, carbohydrate 71g, fat
34g, saturated fat 19g, fiber 5g, added sugar none, salt 0.51g

Chili, lemon, pine nuts and golden raisins
make pasta and cauliflower surprisingly tasty.

# Spicy Cauliflower Pasta

1 medium cauliflower,
cut into small florets
12oz trompetti or other
pasta tubes
4 tbsp olive oil
2 garlic cloves, sliced
1 red chili, seeded and sliced
3oz pine nuts
2oz golden raisins
finely pared zest of 1 lemon,
shredded (or use a zester)
juice of ½ lemon
4 tbsp chopped fresh parsley
salt & pepper to taste
2oz parmesan cheese,
grated (optional)

Takes 20 minutes • Serves 4

1  Cook the cauliflower in salted boiling water for
2 minutes. Drain and rinse with cold water to stop it
cooking further. Drain again. Cook the pasta in salted
boiling water according to the package instructions.
2  Meanwhile, heat the oil in a large frying pan. Add
the cauliflower and fry for 3 minutes until lightly
golden. Reduce the heat, add the garlic, chili and
pine nuts and cook 2 minutes more.
3  Add the drained pasta, golden raisins, lemon zest
and juice and parsley. Season with salt and pepper
and toss together with the parmesan, if using.

• Per serving: 691 calories, protein 22g, carbohydrate 78g, fat
35g, saturated fat 6g, fiber 5g, added sugar none, salt 0.42g

Taleggio is a small rectangular Italian
cheese that melts wonderfully over pasta.

# Pasta with Taleggio

2 tbsp olive oil
1 onion, sliced
1 red, 1 yellow and 1 green pepper,
seeded and sliced
2 garlic cloves, sliced
2 cups crushed tomatoes
12oz rigatoni (ridged pasta tubes)
salt & pepper to taste
pinch of sugar (optional)
handful of fresh basil, torn
9oz taleggio cheese,
thinly sliced

Takes 45 minutes • Serves 4

1  Heat the oil in a large frying pan and saute the
onion for 2–3 minutes. Add the peppers and cook
over medium heat until lightly browned. Reduce the
heat, add the garlic and cook for 2 minutes. Stir in
the crushed tomatoes and ½ cup water. Bring to a
boil and simmer for 15 minutes, until the sauce is
thickened and reduced.
2  Meanwhile, cook the pasta in salted boiling water
according to the package instructions. Preheat the
broiler. Season the sauce with salt and pepper and
add a pinch of sugar, if necessary. Add the drained
pasta and half the basil and spread into a shallow,
flameproof dish.
3  Arrange the cheese over the top and broil for 5
minutes until the cheese is melted. Scatter with the
remaining basil and serve.

• Per serving: 692 calories, protein 15g, carbohydrate 75g, fat
39g, saturated fat 20g, fiber 5g, added sugar 15g, salt 0.59g

Pumpkin can be bland, but here it's spiced up with
chili, sage and lemon zest.

# Ravioli with Pumpkin

1lb2oz package fresh
cheese ravioli
1 tbsp olive oil
1 onion, finely chopped
1 garlic clove, crushed
15oz can solid pumpkin
2oz parmesan cheese,
finely grated
pinch of crushed chili flakes
finely grated zest of 1 lemon
salt & pepper to taste
1oz butter
3oz fresh white breadcrumbs
2 tbsp chopped fresh sage
deep-fried sage leaves, to garnish
(optional)

Takes 30 minutes • Serves 4

1 Cook the ravioli according to the package
instructions. Meanwhile, heat the olive oil in a small
pan and fry the onion and garlic for 2–3 minutes,
until softened. Add the pumpkin, 1 cup water, the
grated parmesan, chili flakes and lemon zest. Stir
well and cook over a low heat for 3–4 minutes.
Season with salt and pepper.
2 In a small frying pan, melt the butter, then stir in
the breadcrumbs and saute until lightly golden. Stir
in the chopped sage.
3 Drain the ravioli and spoon into bowls. Pour over
the pumpkin sauce and sprinkle with the toasted
sage breadcrumbs. Serve with the deep-fried sage,
if liked.

• Per serving: 674 calories, protein 26g, carbohydrate 94g, fat
24g, saturated fat 12g, fiber 5g, added sugar none, salt 1.28g

Don't bother with layering the lasagne in a dish,
this easy version is assembled on the plate.

# Chili Bean Open Lasagne

1 tbsp olive oil
1 onion, chopped
2 garlic cloves, crushed
1 red chili, finely sliced
1 small eggplant, chopped
1 large zucchini, chopped
15oz can borlotti beans, drained
15oz can chopped tomatoes
2 tbsp tomato paste
salt & pepper to taste
8oz pack fresh lasagne sheets
handful of basil, torn
4oz cheddar cheese, grated
green salad, to serve

Takes 30 minutes • Serves 4

1 Heat the oil in a large frying pan. Saute the onion for 3 minutes, until softened. Add the garlic, chili, eggplant and zucchini and saute for a further 2 minutes. Stir in the beans, tomatoes and tomato paste and season with salt and pepper. Bring to a boil and simmer for 5 minutes.

2 Meanwhile, cook the lasagne sheets in salted boiling water according to the package instructions. Drain, then halve each sheet diagonally. Stir all but four of the basil sprigs into the bean mixture.

3 Place a spoonful of the mixture onto each plate and top with a quarter of the lasagne triangles. Top with the remaining bean mix, grated cheese and the basil sprigs. Serve with a green salad.

• Per serving: 400 calories, protein 17g, carbohydrate 73g, fat 6g, saturated fat 1g, fiber 11g, added sugar none, salt 1.21g

*Using fresh pasta in this dish
makes it even easier.*

# Cheese and Tomato Cannelloni

5 tbsp extra virgin olive oil
1lb10oz ripe cherry tomatoes
2 tsp dried oregano
2 tsp fine light brown sugar
salt & pepper to taste
6 tbsp fresh red or green pesto
8oz soft goat's cheese, rind trimmed
12 fresh lasagne sheets
12oz vine-ripe tomatoes,
thinly sliced
3 tbsp freshly grated parmesan
cheese
basil leaves and green salad,
to serve

Takes 1 hour 20 minutes • Serves 4

1  Preheat the oven to 425°F. Oil a shallow baking dish. Halve 9oz of the cherry tomatoes. Heat the oil in a frying pan, add the whole cherry tomatoes, cover and cook over a high heat, shaking the pan, for 5 minutes. Add the oregano and sugar. Season with salt and pepper.

2  Beat the pesto into the goat's cheese. Lay out the lasagne and spread the cheese mixture over each sheet. Top with tomato slices and roll up like a jelly roll. Spoon half the cherry tomato sauce into the dish. Arrange the pasta rolls on top and spoon on any remaining tomato sauce. Scatter the cherry tomato halves on top and cover with foil.

3  Bake for 25–30 minutes. Uncover, sprinkle with the cheese and bake for 10 minutes until brown. Serve with basil and a green salad.

• Per serving: 635 calories, protein 21g, carbohydrate 57g, fat 37g, saturated fat 5g, fiber 6g, added sugar 3g, salt 1.46g

This pasta dish is perfect to have bubbling in
the oven while you chat with your guests.

# Fiorentina Baked Pasta

1 tbsp olive oil
1lb 2oz mushrooms, halved
2 garlic cloves, chopped
salt & pepper to taste
10oz your favorite spinach and
cheese sauce
1 cup milk
2oz parmesan cheese, grated
10oz puntalette (rice-shaped pasta)

Takes 1 hour • Serves 4

1 Preheat the oven to 375°F. Heat the oil in a large
frying pan, add the mushrooms and saute over a
high heat for 5 minutes until lightly golden. Reduce
the heat, add the garlic and cook for 2 minutes.
Season with salt and pepper and place in a shallow
ovenproof dish.
2 Place the spinach sauce, milk, half the parmesan
cheese and pasta in a large bowl. Stir and season
with salt and pepper to taste. Pour over the mushrooms and scatter the remaining parmesan on top.
3 Bake for 45 minutes until the pasta is tender and
most of the liquid has been absorbed.

• Per serving: 594 calories, protein 27g, carbohydrate 67g, fat
26g, saturated fat 12g, fiber 4g, added sugar none, salt 1.56g

Gnocchi are small Italian potato dumplings.
They are treated like pasta and served with a tasty sauce.

# Lemon Butter Gnocchi

15oz fresh potato gnocchi
2 tbsp olive oil
10oz butternut squash,
peeled, halved, seeded
and roughly chopped
1 tsp sugar
finely grated zest of 1 lemon and
½ of the juice
3oz butter
2 tbsp chopped fresh rosemary
salt & pepper to taste
green salad, to serve

Takes 20 minutes • Serves 2

1  Cook the gnocchi according to the package instructions. Meanwhile, heat the oil in a small frying pan and saute the butternut squash for 5 minutes until tender. Sprinkle with the sugar and lemon zest and saute 1 minute more, until slightly caramelized.
2  Melt the butter in a small pan. Stir in the lemon juice and chopped rosemary and season with salt and pepper to taste. Drain the gnocchi and stir into the butternut squash. Stir well to combine.
3  Spoon into warmed serving bowls, then drizzle the lemon and rosemary butter sauce on top. Serve with a green salad.

• Per serving: 615 calories, protein 8g, carbohydrate 63g, fat 39g, saturated fat 21g, fiber 5g, added sugar 3g, salt 0.97g

Potato gnocchi, bought vacuum-packed, make
a great refrigerator or freezer stand-by.

# Gnocchi with Fava Beans

12oz potato gnocchi
2 tbsp olive oil
9oz small mushrooms, halved
2 garlic cloves, crushed
8oz frozen fava beans
3 tbsp chopped fresh tarragon
8oz mascarpone cheese
1 tbsp lemon juice
salt & pepper to taste
parmesan cheese shavings and
shredded lemon zest, to garnish
salad, to serve (optional)

Takes 20 minutes • Serves 4

1  Cook the gnocchi according to the package instructions. Drain and set aside. Heat the oil in a frying pan, add the mushrooms and saute quickly over a high heat until browned. Lift out with a slotted spoon and add to the gnocchi.

2  Wipe out the pan, then add the garlic, beans, tarragon and mascarpone. Heat gently, stirring, until the mascarpone has melted. Add the lemon juice, mushrooms and gnocchi to the pan. Heat through for 1 minute. Season with salt and pepper.

3  Divide among serving plates and scatter on the parmesan shavings and  lemon zest. Serve with salad, if you like.

• Per serving: 488 calories, protein 10g, carbohydrate 28g, fat 38g, saturated fat 20g, fiber 5g, added sugar none, salt 0.54g

This version is cooked in the microwave,
which cuts down the need for stirring.

# Leek and Mushroom Risotto

1oz butter
1 tbsp olive oil
1 leek, cut into thin slices
1 garlic clove, crushed
10oz arborio rice
3 cups hot vegetable stock
salt & pepper to taste
9oz mushrooms, sliced
2oz fresh parmesan cheese, grated
green salad, to serve

Takes 40 minutes • Serves 4

1  Put the butter, oil, leek and garlic into a large bowl. Cover with plastic wrap and cook on High for 5 minutes.
2  Stir the rice into the hot leeks, then stir in the stock and season with salt and pepper. Cook, uncovered, on High for 10 minutes. Throw in the mushrooms, stir and cook on High for 6 minutes.
3  Mix in half the parmesan and leave the risotto to stand for 5 minutes. Serve with a green salad and the remaining parmesan for sprinkling.

• Per serving: 397 calories, protein 13g, carbohydrate 60g, fat 13g, saturated fat 6g, fiber 3g, added sugar none, salt 1.22g

This oven-baked risotto works beautifully and
saves effort, because you don't have to stand over it.

# Baked Spinach Risotto

1oz butter
1 garlic clove, crushed
1 small red onion, chopped
4oz arborio rice
1 tbsp chopped fresh rosemary,
plus extra to garnish
1 cup vegetable stock
9fl oz white wine
10oz antipasto mixed peppers
2oz spinach
1oz parmesan cheese, grated
salt & pepper to taste
green salad, to serve

Takes 55 minutes • Serves 2

1  Preheat the oven to 350°F. Put the butter and
garlic in a 1-quart ovenproof dish and place
in the oven for 2 minutes until the butter has melted.
Add the onion and toss to coat, then return to the
oven for 3–4 minutes more to soften.
2  Add the rice, rosemary, stock and wine and return
to the oven for 30 minutes, stirring once or twice
during cooking.
3  Stir in the antipasto peppers and spinach and
return to the oven for another 10 minutes, until all
the liquid has been absorbed. Stir in the parmesan
and season with salt and pepper. Serve with a fresh
green salad.

• Per serving: 534 calories, protein 11g, carbohydrate 54g, fat
23g, saturated fat 10g, fiber 3g, added sugar none, salt 1.25g

A simple dish, easily varied by adding peas,
fried mushrooms or corn.

# Cheddar and Tomato Rice

2 tbsp oil
1 onion, thinly sliced
1 red pepper, cored, seeded
and sliced
1 garlic clove, finely chopped
10oz long grain rice
3½ cups vegetable stock
8oz can chopped tomatoes
salt & pepper to taste
4oz sharp cheddar cheese, cubed
chives and salad greens, to garnish

Takes 1 hour • Serves 4

1  Preheat the oven to 350°F. Heat the oil in a large flameproof casserole and saute the onion and red pepper over medium heat until golden. Add the chopped garlic and cook for a minute more.
2  Add the rice and stir until completely coated in oil. Add the stock and tomatoes, and season with salt and pepper. Bring to a boil and simmer for 5 minutes, until nearly all the liquid has been absorbed.
3  Scatter with the cheese, cover the casserole and cook in the oven for about 30 minutes, until the rice is tender. Leave for 5 minutes before garnishing with chives and salad leaves.

• Per serving: 463 calories, protein 14g, carbohydrate 72g, fat 15g, saturated fat 6g, fiber 2g, added sugar none, salt 1.32g

Cook the rice earlier in the day, because it
stir fries better when it's cooled first.

# Thai Fried Rice with Vegetables

2 tbsp sunflower oil
1 red chili, finely sliced
1 stalk lemongrass, finely chopped
2 shallots, finely sliced
1 garlic clove, crushed
2in piece fresh ginger,
finely chopped
5oz jasmine rice, cooked
and cooled
1 small red pepper, seeded
and sliced
1 carrot, cut into matchsticks
2 scallions, shredded
3oz snow peas, sliced
1 tbsp light soy sauce
1oz shredded coconut, toasted
fresh cilantro (coriander) leaves

Takes 35 minutes • Serves 2

1  Heat 1 tablespoon of the oil in a wok or large fry-ing pan. Stir fry the chili, lemongrass, shallots, garlic and ginger over low heat for 2 minutes until softened. Add the cooked rice and stir fry, stirring, for 3–4 minutes more.
2  Meanwhile, heat the remaining oil in another f pan and toss in the pepper, carrot, scallions and snow peas. Stir fry for 2–3 minutes.
3  Stir the soy sauce into the rice and spoon into serving bowls. Top with the vegetables, coconut and torn cilantro leaves, and serve.

• Per serving: 930 calories, protein 17g, carbohydrate 177g, fat 22g, saturated fat 6g, fiber 5g, added sugar none, salt 1.17g

You could use leftover rice to make this tasty and colorful Indonesian fried rice, if it has been kept well chilled.

# Spicy Nasi Goreng

10oz long-grain rice, rinsed
2 medium eggs, beaten
3 garlic cloves
2 red chilies, thinly sliced
2 onions, sliced
3 tbsp sunflower oil
1 yellow pepper, seeded and sliced
2 carrots, cut into matchsticks
2 tbsp dark soy sauce
4 scallions, shredded
salt & pepper to taste
4 tbsp chopped fresh cilantro (coriander)

Takes 35 minutes • Serves 2

1  Place the rice in a wok, add 2 cups water and bring to a boil. Cover and cook over a very low heat for 15 minutes, until all the liquid has been absorbed. Put into a shallow dish and leave to cool.
2  Meanwhile, heat the wok. Add the eggs and cook, stirring, until scrambled. Remove and set aside. process the garlic, half the chili and half the onions to a paste in a blender. Heat the oil in the wok and stir fry the paste for 1 minute. Add the rest of the onions and chili, plus the vegetables, and stir fry for 2 minutes.
3  Add the cold rice and stir fry for 3 minutes. Stir in the soy sauce, scallions and eggs and fry until piping hot. Season with salt and pepper and serve immediately.

• Per serving: 445 calories, protein 10g, carbohydrate 72g, fat 15g, saturated fat 3g, fiber 2g, added sugar none, salt 0.16g

A pack of egg noodles is a useful item to have in your pantry. They cook quickly and are good with stir fries as well as in a warm salad.

# Sesame Noodle Salad

5oz medium egg noodles
3 tbsp sesame oil
1 tbsp dark soy sauce
2 tsp lemon juice
1 large carrot, peeled
4in piece cucumber
or zucchini
2 tsp sesame seeds
2 garlic cloves, finely chopped
1oz fresh ginger, peeled
and finely chopped
4 scallions, shredded
½–1 tsp Chinese five-spice powder
handful of arugula
salt & pepper to taste

Takes 15 minutes • Serves 2

1 Cook the noodles according to the package instructions. Rinse in a colander under cold water and drain well. Put into a bowl and add the sesame oil, soy sauce and lemon juice.

2 Use a potato peeler to cut the carrot into fine ribbons. Do the same with the cucumber or zucchini, discarding the central seed section. Add to the noodles.

3 Heat a small pan and dry fry the sesame seeds until pale gold. Sprinkle over the noodles. Add the oil to the pan and stir fry the garlic, ginger, scallions and five-spice powder for 30 seconds. Stir in the arugula. Toss with the noodles, season with salt and pepper and serve.

• Per serving: 655 calories, protein 15g, carbohydrate 58g, fat 42g, saturated fat 5g, fiber 6g, added sugar none, salt 1.47g

Tofu is soy bean curd. It tastes bland but, like chicken,
it is good at absorbing flavors from other ingredients.

# Tofu Chow Mein

8oz egg noodles
1 tbsp vegetable oil
3 scallions, sliced
2 garlic cloves, finely chopped
¾in piece fresh ginger,
peeled and finely chopped
10oz firm tofu, cut into small cubes
8oz can bamboo shoots, sliced
4oz beansprouts
4oz snow peas, sliced lengthwise
2 tbsp soy sauce
2 tbsp sweet chili sauce

Takes 25 minutes • Serves 4

1  Cook the noodles according to the package
instructions. Meanwhile, heat the oil in a large frying
pan or wok and stir fry the scallions, garlic and
ginger for 1–2 minutes, until slightly softened.
2  Add the tofu cubes and stir fry over high heat for
2–3 minutes until golden. Stir in the bamboo shoots,
beansprouts and snow peas and stir fry 1–2
minutes more.
3  Drain the noodles and add to the vegetables with
the soy sauce and chili sauce. Toss together and
serve immediately.

• Per serving: 361 calories, protein 16g, carbohydrate 49g, fat
12g, saturated fat 1g, fiber 4g, added sugar none, salt 1.4g

Look for pre-cooked, vacuum-packed noodles that
can be added straight to the wok without boiling.

# Thai Satay Noodles

3 tbsp crunchy peanut butter
3 tbsp sweet chili sauce
3½fl oz thick coconut milk
3½fl oz vegetable stock
2 tbsp soy sauce
10oz cooked thin egg noodles
2 tbsp sesame oil
2in piece fresh ginger, grated
5oz broccoli florets
1 small red pepper, seeded
and sliced
3oz baby corn, halved lengthwise
2oz snow peas
3 garlic cloves, finely chopped
small handful fresh basil leaves
1oz roasted peanuts,
roughly chopped

Takes 25 minutes • Serves 4

1  Mix the peanut butter, chili sauce, coconut milk,
stock and soy sauce to make a smooth satay sauce.
Gently separate the noodles (you may need to pour
boiling water over them).
2  Heat the oil in a wok and stir fry the ginger,
broccoli, peppers and corn for 3 minutes. Add the
snow peas and garlic and stir fry further 2 minutes
moe. Pour the peanut sauce into the pan and bring
to a boil.
3  Drain the noodles thoroughly. Add to the wok and
stir fry over high heat for 1–2 minutes. Sprinkle with
the basil leaves and peanuts and serve.

• Per serving: 588 calories, protein 18g, carbohydrate 62g, fat
31g, saturated fat 8g, fiber 7g, added sugar none, salt 1.8g

Sweet beets and sharp horseradish
make a delightful flavor contrast.

# Roasted Beets with Horseradish

2lb 4oz fresh, uncooked beets,
peeled and cut into wedges
14oz shallots, halved if large
3 tbsp olive oil
3 tbsp balsamic vinegar
salt & pepper to taste
3 tsp caraway seeds, plus extra
for sprinkling
boiled rice, to serve
handful of fresh chives, to garnish

FOR THE SAUCE
½ cup sour cream
1oz fresh horseradish, grated,
or 2 tbsp hot horseradish
from a jar

Takes 1 hour • Serves 4

1  Preheat the oven to 400°F. Place the bees in a large roasting pan along with the shallots. Drizzle with the olive oil and balsamic vinegar, season with salt and pepper and toss well to coat. Roast for 25 minutes.
2  Add the caraway seeds and toss to mix. Roast 20 minutes more, until the beets is tender and the shallots are softened and golden.
3  Mix together the sour cream and horseradish and season with salt and pepper. Serve the roasted vegetables with plain boiled rice. Spoon over the sour cream mixture and garnish with the caraway seeds and fresh chives.

• Per serving: 256 calories, protein 9g, carbohydrate 28g, fat 13g, saturated fat 2g, fiber 7g, added sugar none, salt 0.53g

Quick-cook polenta is a great midweek standby.
Quark is a piquant cow's milk curd cheese.

# Spring Vegetable Polenta

### FOR THE POLENTA
3 cups vegetable stock
6oz quick-cook polenta
4oz quark
4oz pesto sauce
salt & pepper to taste
parmesan cheese shavings,
to serve (optional)

### FOR THE VEGETABLES
4oz baby corn, halved lengthwise
4oz baby carrots, trimmed
4oz green beans,
trimmed and thickly sliced
4oz fresh (or frozen) peas
finely pared zest of
1 lemon, chopped
2 tbsp chopped fresh parsley
1 garlic clove, finely chopped

Takes 15 minutes • Serves 4

1 In a large pot, bring the stock to a rolling boil and sprinkle in the polenta in a steady stream, whisking continuously, until thickened. Stir in the quark and cook over low heat for 5 minutes, stirring occasionally.
2 Meanwhile, steam the vegetables for 3–4 minutes. Remove the polenta from the heat and beat in the pesto sauce. Season with salt and pepper to taste. Spoon on to warmed serving plates.
3 Serve the vegetables on top of the polenta. Scatter the lemon zest, parsley and garlic on top and serve immediately with freshly shaved vegetarian parmesan, if you like.

• Per serving: 394 calories, protein 15g, carbohydrate 40g, fat 21g, saturated fat 3g, fiber 4g, added sugar none, salt 1.27g

Serve this saucy curry in deep bowls with spoonfuls
of cooling sour cream and warm bread for dunking.

# Pumpkin and Apple Curry

1 tbsp sunflower oil
1 large onion, roughly chopped
3 garlic cloves, chopped
1lb 2oz pumpkin, peeled,
seeded and cubed
1lb 12oz baking potatoes, cubed
1 medium cooking apple, peeled,
cored and diced
2 tsp mild curry paste
1 tsp turmeric
1in fresh ginger, chopped
2 bay leaves
1 vegetable stock cube
2oz raisins
salt & pepper to taste
4 tbsp sour cream, to serve
bread or rice, to serve

Takes 45 minutes • Serves 4

1 Heat the oil in a pan, add the onion and saute for
5 minutes until golden. Add the garlic, pumpkin,
potatoes and apple. Stir in the curry paste, turmeric,
ginger and bay leaves.
2 Add 18fl oz water, the stock cube, raisins and
plenty of salt and pepper. Bring to a boil, stirring.
Cover and simmer for 15 minutes, stirring
occasionally, until the vegetables are tender.
3 Spoon into bowls and top with the sour cream
and a pinch of turmeric. Serve with bread or rice.

• Per serving: 270 calories, protein 5g, carbohydrate 55g, fat
5g, saturated fat 1g, fiber 6g, added sugar none, salt 0.23g

*A filling tart, delicious served
hot or cold with salads.*

# Potato and Onion Tart

13oz ready-made pie crust,
thawed if frozen
2 tbsp olive oil
1lb onions, thinly sliced
2 garlic cloves, crushed
3 tbsp fresh thyme leaves or
1 tbsp dried
1lb 10oz starchy potatoes,
peeled and thickly sliced
2 eggs
7oz crème fraîche (or cream mixed
with 1/2 tsp buttermilk)
2 tbsp wholegrain mustard
salt & pepper to taste
salad, to serve

Takes 50 minutes • Serves 4

1  Preheat the oven to 425°F. Use the pie crust to line the base and sides of a flat cookie pan about 9 × 13 inches. Heat the oil in a large frying pan and saute the onions for 8–10 minutes, until just beginning to caramelize. Stir in the garlic and most of the thyme and cook 2 minutes more. Scatter half over the pie crust.
2  Parboil the potatoes in salted boiling water for 4–5 minutes. Drain well and arrange in the pan. Scatter with the remaining onions.
3  Beat together the eggs, crème fraîche and mustard. Season well with salt and pepper and pour over the vegetables. Scatter the rest of the thyme on top and bake the tart for 20 minutes, until the filling has set and is golden. Serve with a salad.

• Per serving: 706 calories, protein 14g, carbohydrate 84g, fat 37g, saturated fat 14g, fiber 6g, added sugar none, salt 0.84g

A substantial main course salad with spiced canned
chickpeas and naan bread croutons.

# Indian Chickpea Salad

6 tbsp olive oil
3 garlic cloves, sliced
2 red chilies, seeded and sliced
4 tsp cumin seeds, lightly crushed
2 × 15oz cans chickpeas, drained
and rinsed
3 tomatoes, halved, seeded
and diced
shredded zest and juice of 1 lemon
salt & pepper to taste
1 naan bread

FOR THE SALAD
1oz fresh cilantro (coriander)
½ cucumber, cut into sticks
1 medium red onion, sliced
4oz baby spinach leaves

Takes 30 minutes • Serves 4

1  Put 5 tablespoons of the oil in a pan. Add the garlic, chilies and cumin and warm over medium heat
for 10 minutes. Take care not to burn the
garlic. Add the chickpeas and heat through for 5
minutes. Meanwhile, preheat the broiler.
2  Add the tomatoes, lemon zest and juice to the
chickpeas. Season with salt and pepper and set
aside. Brush the naan bread with the remaining
oil and broil both sides until crisp. Tear into bite-size
pieces.
3  Toss together the salad ingredients and divide
among serving plates. Spoon on the chickpeas and
top with the naan bread croutons.

• Per serving: 641 calories, protein 23g, carbohydrate 66g, fat
33g, saturated fat 6g, fiber 11g, added sugar 0.2g, salt 0.65g

Couscous only needs to be soaked before you eat it,
so it's a quick accompaniment to colorful roasted vegetables.

# Roasted Vegetable Couscous

1 red and 1 yellow pepper,
seeded and diced
2 zucchini, diced
1 eggplant, diced
1 red onion, chopped
2 garlic cloves, chopped
1 tbsp fresh rosemary, chopped
5 tbsp olive oil
salt & pepper to taste
9oz couscous
15oz flageolet or navy beans,
drained and rinsed
2 tbsp balsamic vinegar
green salad, to serve

Takes 45 minutes • Serves 4

1  Preheat the oven to 425°F. Place all the vegetables, garlic and rosemary in a large roasting pan and drizzle with 4 tablespoons oil. Season with salt and pepper and roast for 20 minutes, stirring after 10 minutes.
2  Meanwhile, put the couscous in a bowl and add 14fl oz boiling water. Season with salt and pepper and leave for 20 minutes until all the water has been absorbed. Add the flageolet beans and vinegar to the roasting pan, mix well and roast 10 minutes more.
3  Fluff up the couscous with a fork. Divide among serving plates and top with the roasted vegetable and bean mixture. Serve with a green salad.

• Per serving: 478 calories, protein 15g, carbohydrate 61g, fat 21g, saturated fat 3g, fiber 7g, added sugar none, salt 0.06g

Most melting cheeses will taste great broiled on top of eggplant slices. Try using brie for a change.

# Eggplant with Goat's Cheese

4 medium eggplants, halved lengthwise
3½fl oz olive oil
salt & pepper to taste
2 tbsp sundried tomato paste
1oz fresh basil leaves
4 × 2oz individual, rinded goat's cheeses
1 tbsp white wine vinegar
1 tsp Dijon mustard
pinch of fine sugar
6 oz mixed salad greens
5oz couscous
3oz radishes, halved
crusty bread, to serve

Takes 25 minutes • Serves 4

1 Preheat the broiler. Brush the eggplant halves with 3 tablespoons of the oil and season with salt and pepper. Place the eggplants, cut side up, on a baking sheet and broil for 7 minutes. Turn them over and broil 5 minutes more, until lightly scorched.
2 Spread the cut sides with the tomato paste and arrange the basil leaves on top. Slice each cheese into four rounds and arrange on the eggplants. Season with salt and pepper and broil until bubbling.
3 Whisk the remaining oil, vinegar, mustard and sugar in a salad bowl. Toss the salad in the dressing until coated. Divide among serving plates and arrange the cheesy eggplant halves on top. Serve with crusty bread.

• Per serving: 416 calories, protein 12g, carbohydrate 10g, fat 37g, saturated fat 4g, fiber 7g, added sugar none, salt 2.36g

Paneer is a hard Indian cheese that
melts deliciously into the sauce.

# Pea and Paneer Curry

2 tbsp vegetable oil
8oz paneer, torn into pieces
1 onion, thinly sliced
2 tbsp mild curry paste
1lb potatoes, peeled and
cut into chunks
15oz chopped tomatoes
with garlic
1 cup vegetable stock
10oz frozen peas
salt & pepper to taste
boiled rice, to serve

Takes 45 minutes • Serves 4

1  Heat 1 tablespoon oil in a large saucepan. Saute
the paneer for 2–3 minutes, stirring, until crisp and
golden. Remove with a slotted spoon and set aside.
2  Saute the onion in the remaining oil for
4–5 minutes, until soft and just beginning to brown.
Add the curry paste. Cook, stirring, for 2 minutes.
3  Add the potatoes, tomatoes, stock and paneer,
bring to a boil and simmer for 15 minutes. Add the
peas, bring to a boil again and simmer for 5
minutes. Season with salt and pepper to taste and
serve with boiled rice.

• Per serving: 404 calories, protein 20g, carbohydrate 32g, fat
22g, saturated fat 9g, fiber 7g, added sugar none, salt 2.84g

This is a really tasty supper dish, and it's
easily doubled to feed those hungry hordes.

# Tomato and Goat's Cheese Crumble

2lb 4oz ripe tomatoes,
preferably a mixture, including
some cherry tomatoes
5 tbsp olive oil
salt & pepper to taste
8oz goat's cheese, firm or soft
2oz pine nuts
4oz fresh white breadcrumbs
2oz parmesan cheese,
freshly grated
green salad or vegetables, to serve

Takes 55 minutes • Serves 4

1 Preheat the oven to 375°F. Chop the tomatoes, keeping the cherry ones whole. Heat 2 tablespoons of olive oil in a pan, add the chopped tomatoes, season with salt and pepper and cook for 10 minutes, until softened, stirring occasionally. Remove from the heat and stir in the cherry tomatoes.
2 Spoon half the tomatoes into a 1-quart ovenproof dish and crumble half the goat's cheese on top. Repeat the layers.
3 Heat 3 tablespoons of olive oil in a frying pan and lightly fry the pine nuts and breadcrumbs. Remove from the heat and stir in half the parmesan. Scatter over the tomatoes and cheese and top with the remaining parmesan. Bake for 20–25 minutes, until golden. Serve with a green salad or vegetables.

• Per serving: 431 calories, protein 22g, carbohydrate 28g, fat 27g, saturated fat 12g, fiber 3g, added sugar none, salt 1.78g

Instead of using bread dough, this pizza crust is made from quick-cook polenta spread on a baking tray.

# Polenta Pizza

8oz quick-cook polenta
salt & pepper to taste
2oz parmesan cheese, grated
1 tbsp olive oil
1 red onion, sliced
2 garlic cloves, sliced
1 zucchini, sliced
4oz mushrooms, sliced
4 ripe plum tomatoes, sliced
4oz mozzarella cheese, thinly sliced
1 tbsp green pesto
green salad, to serve

Takes 50 minutes • Serves 4

1  Cook the polenta according to the package instructions. Season well with salt and pepper and stir in the parmesan. Pour on to an oiled baking sheet, spread out to an 11-inch circle and leave to firm up for 15 minutes. Meanwhile, preheat the oven to 400°F.

2  Heat the oil in a large frying pan and saute the onion for 5 minutes, until softened. Add the garlic and zucchini and cook 2 minutes more. Season with salt and pepper and scatter on the polenta crust, along with the mushrooms and tomatoes.

3  Arrange the mozzarella on top and dot with the pesto. Bake for 20 minutes, until the cheese has melted. Serve cut in wedges with a green salad.

• Per serving: 423 calories, protein 19g, carbohydrate 50g, fat 18g, saturated fat 7g, fiber 53g, added sugar none, salt 0.83g

Simple root vegetables combine with
blue cheese to make a satisfying supper.

# Blue Cheese Vegetable Gratin

1lb each of potatoes, carrots
and parsnips, thickly sliced
bunch of scallions
large knob of butter
5oz stilton or any blue cheese
green beans, to serve

Takes 40 minutes • Serves 4

1  Preheat the oven to 400°F. Cook the potatoes,
carrots and parsnips in salted boiling water for
8–10 minutes, until just tender. Drain well.
2  Roughly chop the scallions. Melt the butter in the
pan you cooked the vegetables in (no need to wash
it), add the scallions and saute gently for a minute or
two, until softened slightly. Add the vegetables and
stir gently until coated with butter. Put in a buttered,
shallow ovenproof dish.
3  Slice the cheese and arrange over the top of the
vegetables. Bake for 20 minutes, until the cheese
has melted. Serve hot, straight from the oven, with
green beans.

• Per serving: 372 calories, protein 13g, carbohydrate 43g, fat
17g, saturated fat 10g, fiber 10g, added sugar none, salt 0.44g

This layered vegetable "cake" makes a perfect alternative
to a roast of meat. Serve with a veggie-friendly gravy.

# Root Vegetable Bake

4oz butter, softened
finely grated zest of 1 small lemon
2 garlic cloves, crushed
3 tbsp fresh thyme leaves
3oz gruyère cheese, finely grated
salt & pepper to taste
1lb10oz firm potatoes, peeled
8oz celeriac, peeled
1lb carrots, peeled
1lb parsnips, peeled
and cored
vegetarian gravy, to serve

Takes 2 hours • Serves 6

1  Preheat the oven to 375ºF. Use 1oz butter to grease an 8-inch cake pan. Mash the remaining butter with the lemon zest, garlic, thyme and gruyère. Season with salt and pepper.
2  Very thinly slice the vegetables. Layer one third of the potatoes, then celeriac, carrots and parsnips in the pan. Dot with the butter. Repeat the layers. Finish with black pepper and dots of butter.
3  Cover the pan with foil and bake for 45 minutes. Remove the foil and bake for 45 minutes more, until the vegetables are tender. Leave for 5 minutes. Invert on to a warm plate, place a plate over the top and invert again so the crispy side is on top. Serve with vegetarian gravy.

• Per serving: 483 calories, protein 38g, carbohydrate 46g, fat 18g, saturated fat 5g, fiber 8g, added sugar none, salt 8.3g

Choose a soft, rindless goat's cheese
for this recipe.

# Leek and Goat's Cheese Tarts

9oz ready-made pie crust
1 tbsp olive oil
1 leek, halved lengthwise and cut
½in pieces
1 yellow pepper, seeded
and chopped
6 pitted black olives, quartered
2 tbsp fresh thyme leaves
4oz soft, rindless goat's
cheese, cubed
green salad or steamed greens,
to serve (optional)

Takes 45 minutes • Serves 4

1  Preheat the oven to 350°F. Roll out the pastry on a lightly floured surface and use it to line four 4½-inch fluted tart pans with removable bottoms. Prick the crust, line with baking parchment and fill with dry beans. Bake for 12 minutes.
2  Meanwhile, heat the oil in a large frying pan and saute the leek and pepper until softened. Remove the paper and beans from the tarts. Fill each tart with the leek and pepper mixture. Scatter on the olives, thyme and goat's cheese.
3  Cook for 10–12 minutes, until the pastry is golden and the cheese is slightly melted. Serve immediately with mixed salad leaves or freshly steamed greens, if you like.

• Per serving: 441 calories, protein 9g, carbohydrate 38g, fat 29g, saturated fat 11g, fiber 3g, added sugar none, salt 1.68g

Frozen puff pastry makes a quick crust
for a tangy, salty filling.

# Red Onion, Feta and Olive Tart

1oz butter
2 large red onions, finely sliced
2 tbsp light brown sugar
2 tbsp balsamic vinegar
flour, for dusting
16oz puff pastry, thawed if frozen
4oz feta cheese, crumbled
6oz black olives, pitted
and chopped
salt & pepper to taste
1 tbsp extra virgin olive oil
shredded basil leaves, to garnish
green salad, to serve

Takes 45 minutes • Serves 4

1 Preheat the oven to 400°F. Heat the butter in a pan and add the onions. Add a pinch of salt and saute for about 10 minutes, until caramelized. Add the sugar and balsamic vinegar and cook 5 minutes more, until the juices are reduced and syrupy. Leave to cool.

2 Roll out the pastry on a floured surface and use it to line a 12 × 8½-inch flat cookie pan. Cover with the onion mixture and scatter the feta and olives on top. Season with salt and pepper and drizzle on the olive oil.

3 Bake for 15–20 minutes until the pastry is risen and golden and the crust is crisp. Scatter the basil leaves and cut into wedges. Serve with a green salad.

• Per serving: 646 calories, protein 11g, carbohydrate 53g, fat 44g, saturated fat 18g, fiber 2g, added sugar 8g, salt 4.07g

Buy a ready-made pie crust to save time.
Try asparagus instead of the scallions for a milder flavor.

# Cheesy Scallion Tart

bunch scallions, trimmed
1 tbsp olive oil
8oz soft goat's cheese, rind removed
½ cup heavy cream
3 eggs, separated
9½in ready-made pie crust
tomato salad, to serve

Takes 40 minutes • Serves 6

1 Preheat the oven to 375°F and preheat the broiler. Place the scallions on a baking sheet and brush with the oil. Broil for 2 minutes.
2 In a bowl, beat together the goat's cheese, cream and egg yolks until smooth. Whisk the egg whites until stiff and gently fold into the cheese mixture. Spoon into the crust and arrange the scallions on top.
3 Bake for 20–25 minutes, until golden. Serve with a tomato salad.

• Per serving: 337 calories, protein 11g, carbohydrate 18g, fat 25g, saturated fat 13g, fiber 1g, added sugar 3g, salt 0.64g

The curry paste is hot, but the yogurt
and chutney cool it right down.

# Creamy Egg Curry

2 tbsp oil
1 large, or 2 medium onions
(about 10oz total weight),
thinly sliced
2 heaped tbsp curry paste
230g can tomatoes
salt & pepper to taste
8 eggs
5oz frozen peas
4 tbsp plain, mild yogurt
cooked rice and mango chutney,
to serve

Takes 45 minutes • Serves 4

1  Heat the oil in a frying pan. Add the onion and cook for 10 minutes until golden. Add the curry paste and cook, stirring, for 2 minutes. Add the tomatoes, 7fl oz water and season with salt and pepper. Bring to a boil, then simmer for 20 minutes. Add a splash of water if the curry becomes too thick.

2  Meanwhile, boil the eggs for 8 minutes.

3  Stir the peas and yogurt into the curry. Simmer for 2–3 minutes. Peel and halve each egg and gently stir into the curry. Serve with cooked rice and mango chutney.

• Per serving: 302 calories, protein 18g, carbohydrate 12g, fat 21g, saturated fat 5g, fiber 3g, added sugar none, salt 0.84g

This rustic, peasant-style salad, traditional to southern Italy, is packed with the flavor of sun-ripened vegetables.

# Tuscan Salad

2 red peppers, seeded and quartered
2 yellow peppers, seeded and quartered
1 ciabatta loaf
6 tbsp extra virgin olive oil
3 tbsp red wine vinegar
2 garlic cloves, crushed
salt & pepper to taste
6 ripe plum tomatoes, cut into chunks
2oz caper berries or capers
2oz marinated black olives
handful of fresh basil leaves, roughly torn
2 tbsp pine nuts, toasted

Takes 35 minutes • Serves 4

1 Preheat the broiler. Broil the peppers until charred all over and place in a plastic bag so that the steam loosens the skins.

2 Meanwhile, tear the bread into rough chunks, toast until golden brown and place in a large bowl. Beat together the olive oil, vinegar and garlic, season the dressing with salt and pepper, and set aside.

3 Remove the skin from the peppers and cut into chunks. Toss with the toasted bread, along with the tomatoes, caper berries or capers, olives, basil, pine nuts and the dressing. Serve immediately on its own or as an accompaniment to a creamy goat cheese or ripe brie.

• Per serving: 622 calories, protein 15g, carbohydrate 69g, fat 33g, saturated fat 4g, fiber 5g, added sugar none, salt 2.68g

Crisp, crunchy textures with fresh flavors
will make this speedy salad a certain favorite.

# Orange and Celery Salad

2 large oranges
1 small head celery (about 12oz),
separated into stalks, trimmed,
destringed and sliced
on the diagonal
1 small red onion, cut into
very thin wedges
8oz red cherry tomatoes, halved
3oz cress or loose leaf lettuce
1 small garlic clove, crushed
2 tbsp chopped fresh mint
6 tbsp olive oil
1 tbsp balsamic vinegar
salt & pepper to taste

Takes 15 minutes • Serves 4

1  Cut away the peel and pith from the oranges.
Separate into individual segments. Do this over a
bowl to catch the juices.
2  Place the orange segments in a large serving
bowl and add the sliced celery, onion wedges,
tomato halves and lettuce.
3  Add the garlic, mint, olive oil and balsamic vinegar
to the orange juice and whisk until well
combined. Season with salt and pepper to taste and
pour over the salad. Toss well just before serving.

• Per serving: 249 calories, protein 2g, carbohydrate 9g, fat
23g, saturated fat 3g, fiber 3g, added sugar none, salt 0.19g

A colorful winter salad
with a deliciously nutty dressing.

# Warm Red Cabbage Salad

1 tbsp sunflower oil
1 red onion, sliced
1 small red cabbage (about 12oz), finely shredded
1 red apple, cored and cut into chunks
1 carrot, grated
2 tbsp balsamic vinegar
½ tsp light brown sugar
½ tsp wholegrain mustard
4 tbsp walnut oil
salt & pepper to taste
1 head Boston lettuce, roughly torn
2oz walnut pieces
fresh flatleaf parsley, to garnish

Takes 25 minutes • Serves 4

1  Heat the oil in a frying pan and saute the onion for 1–2 minutes. Add the cabbage and cook 2–3 minutes more. Remove from the heat and add the apple and carrot.
2  Meanwhile, in a small bowl whisk together the vinegar, sugar, mustard and walnut oil. Season the dressing with salt and pepper.
3  Arrange the lettuce leaves on individual serving plates. Spoon the warm cabbage salad over. Sprinkle with the walnut pieces and drizzle with the dressing. Garnish with flatleaf parsley and serve.

• Per serving: 304 calories, protein 4g, carbohydrate 10g, fat 28g, saturated fat 3g, fiber 4g, added sugar 1g, salt 0.09g

Use buckwheat soba noodles for extra flavor and color,
although egg noodles would be good, too.

# Noodle and Watercress Salad

8oz dried buckwheat
soba noodles
2 tbsp light soy sauce
2 tbsp sesame oil
4 tbsp saké (Japanese rice wine) or
dry white wine
2 tsp fine sugar
8 fresh mint leaves
1 large firm mango, peeled, halved,
and pit removed
3oz watercress, stalks removed
2 tbsp sesame seeds, toasted
squeeze of lime juice

Takes 20 minutes • Serves 4

1 Cook the noodles in lightly salted boiling water according to the package instructions, then drain and plunge immediately into cold water to refresh and stop the cooking process. Put the soy sauce, sesame oil, saké and sugar in a small pan and heat gently. Remove from the heat and stir in the mint. Set aside and allow to infuse.

2 Meanwhile, cut the mango into fine slivers. Drain the noodles thoroughly and toss with the soy sauce dressing, mango, watercress and half the sesame seeds.

3 Divide among four serving plates and sprinkle with the remaining sesame seeds. Squeeze on a little lime juice and serve immediately.

• Per serving: 388 calories, protein 9g, carbohydrate 53g, fat 16g, saturated fat 2g, fiber 2g, added sugar 3g, salt 0.04g

A delicious combination of roasted fennel and zesty orange,
served on a bed of herbed wheat.

# Cracked Wheat and Fennel Salad

9oz bulghar wheat
3 heads of fennel, cut into wedges
4 tbsp olive oil
salt & pepper to taste
shredded zest and juice
of 2 oranges
4 tbsp chopped fresh flatleaf parsley
2 tbsp chopped fresh mint
4 plum tomatoes, cut into wedges
5oz mixed olives, drained
4oz arugula

Takes 45 minutes • Serves 4

1 Preheat the oven to 400°F. Place the bulghar wheat in a large bowl, cover with 3½ cups boiling water and allow to stand for 30 minutes. Meanwhile, place the fennel on a large roasting pan, drizzle with the olive oil and season with salt and pepper. Add the orange zest and half the orange juice and roast in the oven for 35 minutes, until softened and slightly charred.

2 Drain the bulghar wheat, add the parsley and mint and remaining orange juice. Combine well and season with salt and pepper. Place the tomatoes, olives and arugula in a large bowl, add the roasted fennel with the pan juices, and toss well.

3 Divide the bulghar wheat among four serving plates, top with the fennel and tomato mixture, and serve.

• Per serving: 422 calories, protein 9g, carbohydrate 53g, fat 39g, saturated fat 5g, fiber 8g, added sugar none, salt 0.03g

So simple to make—serve this fresh-tasting pâté with crusty bread for a snack or light lunch.

# Minty Fava Bean Pâté

1lb 2oz shelled fava beans, outer skins removed
1 garlic clove, very finely chopped
½ cup extra virgin olive oil, plus extra for drizzling
pinch of ground cumin
small bunch fresh mint, chopped
salt & pepper to taste
8 slices crusty wholegrain bread, to serve

Takes 20 minutes, plus resting • Serves 4

1  Cook the beans in lightly salted boiling water for 10–12 minutes, until tender. Drain well, reserving the cooking water. Transfer the beans to a food processor, add the garlic and process to a purée, adding a few tablespoonfuls of the cooking water to give a soft consistency.
2  Preheat the broiler. Transfer the purée to a bowl and stir in the oil, cumin and mint. Season generously with salt and pepper. Set aside for 30 minutes, if possible, to allow the flavors time to develop.
3  Toast each slice of bread on both sides and cut in half. Arrange on individual serving plates. Spoon the pâté on to the hot toast and drizzle on a little extra virgin olive oil.

• Per serving: 413 calories, protein 7g, carbohydrate 9g, fat 39g, saturated fat 5g, fiber 8g, added sugar none, salt 0.03g

If you haven't got a griddle pan, simply stir fry the vegetables
and toast the bagel under a hot broiler.

# Bagels with Grilled Vegetables

5 tbsp olive oil
2 red peppers, seeded and
cut into chunks
2 zucchini, cut into thin slices
on the diagonal
4 onion bagels, split
2 tbsp balsamic vinegar
½ tsp sugar
salt & pepper to taste
2oz arugula

Takes 15 minutes • Serves 4

1  Brush a preheated griddle pan with a little of the oil. Add the peppers and zucchini and cook for 4–5 minutes, turning, until pleasantly charred. Transfer to a plate.
2  Toast the bagels, cut side down, on the hot griddle pan for 1 minute, until golden. Meanwhile, to make a dressing, whisk the vinegar, sugar and remaining oil together. Season with salt and pepper.
3  Place the bagels on individual serving plates and top with the charbroiled vegetables and a handful of arugula. Drizzle the dressing on top and serve immediately.

• Per serving: 330 calories, protein 7g, carbohydrate 32g, fat 20g, saturated fat 3g, fiber 3g, added sugar 1g, salt 0.72g

Focaccia is a flat Italian bread, like the crust of a pizza, often sold flavored with herbs, olives or sundried tomatoes.

# Stuffed Focaccia

15oz can chickpeas, drained and rinsed
juice of 1 lemon
1 garlic clove
5 tbsp extra virgin olive oil
salt & pepper to taste
8-in focaccia with tomatoes
4oz sundried tomatoes in oil, drained
2oz marinated black olives, pitted
large handful mixed salad greens
1 small ripe avocado, halved, peeled and cut into chunks

Takes 15 minutes, plus chilling • Serves 6

1  Put the chickpeas, half the lemon juice and garlic in a food processor and process until smooth. With the motor still running, drizzle in the oil in a steady stream until combined. Season with salt and pepper to taste.

2  Cut the focaccia into three horizontal layers of the same thickness. Spread the chick pea mixture over the bottom two layers and then scatter the sundried tomatoes, olives and salad greens.

3  Toss the avocado with the remaining lemon juice and season with salt and pepper. Scatter over the topping, then reassemble the focaccia. Chill for at least 15 minutes before cutting into wedges to serve.

• Per serving: 305 calories, protein 8g, carbohydrate 27g, fat 19g, saturated fat 2g, fiber 4g, added sugar none, salt 1.27g

The breadcrumb mixture will keep in an airtight container for up to two days. Just reheat it in a dry frying pan.

# Walnut and Broccoli Spaghetti

12oz spaghetti
225g/8oz broccoli, broken into florets
4 tbsp olive oil
1 small onion, chopped
1 garlic clove, crushed
2oz walnuts, chopped
2oz fresh white breadcrumbs
½–1 tsp dried chili flakes
1 tbsp walnut oil

Takes 20 minutes • Serves 4

1  Cook the spaghetti in lightly salted boiling water for 5 minutes. Add the broccoli to the pot, return to a boil and cook 5 minutes more until both are tender.
2  Meanwhile, heat half the oil in a frying pan, add the onion and garlic and cook for 2 minutes, until softened. Add the walnuts, breadcrumbs, dried chili flakes and walnut oil and cook, stirring, until the crumbs are crisp and golden brown.
3  Drain the pasta and broccoli in a colander. Return to the pot, add the remaining olive oil and stir to combine. Divide among individual serving plates. Scatter the breadcrumb mixture on top and serve immediately.

• Per serving: 633 calories, protein 17g, carbohydrate 79g, fat 30g, saturated fat 3g, fiber 5g, added sugar none, salt 0.31g

You can use any pasta shape, but if you cant get
any fresh pasta, use 12oz of dried pasta.

## Pasta with Spicy Peas

3 tbsp olive oil
10oz shallots, halved
4 tsp cumin seeds, lightly crushed
3 garlic cloves, sliced
10oz cherry tomatoes, halved
good splash of Tabasco sauce
14oz frozen baby peas, thawed
finely shredded zest and juice
of ½ lemon
salt & pepper to taste
1lb 2oz fresh penne
4 tbsp chopped parsley

Takes 25 minutes • Serves 4

1  Heat the oil in a large pan. Add the shallots and
cook for about 8 minutes, until softened and lightly
colored. Add the cumin and garlic and cook for 2
minutes more.
2  Stir in the cherry tomatoes and cook for 5
minutes, until softened. Add the Tabasco sauce,
peas and lemon zest and juice. Season with salt and
pepper and cook for 2–3 minutes.
3  Meanwhile, cook the pasta according to the
package instructions and drain. Add the pasta to the
peas and stir until well combined. Stir in the parsley
and serve.

• Per serving: 650 calories, protein 23g, carbohydrate 110g, fat
16g, saturated fat 2g, fiber 11g, added sugar none, salt 0.13g

Big on flavor but short on effort, this dish is
suitable for vegans if you use egg-free pasta.

# Pasta with Eggplant

5 tbsp olive oil, plus extra to serve
2 medium eggplants, diced
2 garlic cloves, finely chopped
2 tsp cumin seeds
1 red chili, seeded and finely sliced
salt & pepper to taste
2oz pine nuts, toasted
2oz golden raisins
12oz tagliatelle (thin
pasta ribbons)
6 tbsp chopped fresh cilantro
(coriander)
zest and juice of 1 lemon
broiled lemon halves, to serve
(optional)

Takes 25 minutes • Serves 4

1 Heat the oil in a large frying pan. Add the eggplants and cook gently, stirring occasionally, for 10
minutes until golden. Add the garlic, cumin and chili,
and cook 4–5 minutes more. Season with salt and
pepper to taste, and add the pine nuts and raisins.
2 Meanwhile, cook the pasta in lightly salted boiling
water, according to the package instructions.
3 Drain the pasta thoroughly and add to the eggplant mixture, along with the cilantro and lemon zest
and juice. Toss and serve with an extra drizzle of
olive oil and broiled lemon halves, if you like.

• Per serving: 627 calories, protein 15g, carbohydrate 79g, fat
30g, saturated fat 4g, fiber 6g, added sugar none, salt 0.07g

This simple Thai dish of noodles and vegetables in a tasty broth makes a satisfying supper.

# Tom Yam Noodles

1 tbsp sunflower oil
1 small onion, chopped
2 garlic cloves
5oz mushrooms, sliced
1 red pepper, seeded and sliced
2 tsp Thai red curry paste
2½ cups vegetable stock
1 tbsp soy sauce
zest of 1 lime and half the juice
4½oz egg noodles
7oz can bamboo shoots, drained
handful of fresh cilantro (coriander)
salt & pepper to taste

1  Heat the oil in a pot and saute the onion until golden. Stir in the garlic, mushrooms and red pepper and saute for 3 minutes. Add the Thai curry paste and cook for 1 minute. Stir in the stock, soy sauce and grated lime zest. Simmer for 3 minutes.
2  Add the noodles to the pot and bring to a boil. Simmer for 4 minutes, until they are cooked. Add the bamboo shoots and most of the coriander and cook for 2 minutes.
3  Divide the noodles between two soup bowls. Add the lime juice to the broth and season with salt and pepper. Pour over the noodles, scatter the remaining coriander on top and serve.

• Per serving: 393 calories, protein 15g, carbohydrate 55g, fat 14g, saturated fat 1g, fiber 7g, added sugar none, salt 2.77g

Takes 35 minutes • Serves 2

This salad is a riot of colors and contrasting textures and it's easily adapted to whatever vegetables you have on hand.

# Warm Crispy Noodle Salad

sunflower oil for deep frying
2oz thin rice noodles
1 tbsp oil
1in piece fresh ginger, chopped
2 garlic cloves, crushed
4oz sugarsnap peas, sliced lengthwise
1 carrot, cut into matchsticks
4 scallions, sliced
6oz spinach leaves, shredded
4oz beansprouts
½ small cucumber, cut into matchsticks
salt & pepper to taste
2oz roasted cashew nuts, chopped
juice of 1 lime
2 tsp chili oil

Takes 30 minutes • Serves 2

1  Pout oil into a pan to a depth of 2 inches and heat until a cube of bread browns in 30 seconds. Carefully add the noodles, a few at a time, and fry for a few seconds until puffed and crisp. Remove and drain on paper towels.

2  Heat 1 tablespoon of oil in a wok, add the ginger and garlic, and stir fry for 30 seconds. Add the sugarsnap peas, carrot and scallions and stir fry for 1 minute. Add the spinach and beansprouts and cook 1 minute more, until wilted.

3  Remove from the heat, stir in the cucumber and season with salt and pepper. Divide between serving plates and scatter the nuts and crispy noodles on top. Squeeze on the lime juice, drizzle with chili oil and serve.

• Per serving: 458 calories, protein 14g, carbohydrate 37g, fat 29g, saturated fat 2g, fiber 6g, added sugar none, salt 0.6g

A simple way to make everyday
vegetables taste out of the ordinary.

# Spicy Coconut Vegetables

1 tbsp olive oil
1 onion, cut into wedges
1 red onion, cut into wedges
1 small red chili, seeded
and chopped
2 carrots, sliced
8oz small broccoli florets
1 red and 1 yellow pepper, seeded
and cut into chunks
7fl oz sweetened condensed
coconut milk
7fl oz vegetable stock
½ tsp Tabasco sauce
jasmine rice, to serve

Takes 25 minutes • Serves 4

1  Heat the olive oil in a large pan and saute the onion wedges and chili for 1–2 minutes, stirring occasionally.
2  Add the carrots, broccoli and peppers and cook for 5 minutes more.
3  Stir in the coconut milk, stock and Tabasco sauce, reduce the heat and simmer for 5 minutes. Serve immediately with rice.

• Per serving: 400 calories, protein 7g, carbohydrate 14g, fat 36g, saturated fat 27g, fiber 11g, added sugar none, salt 0.27g

This chili uses ready-made sweet red pepper sauce,
available at most supermarkets.

# Bean and Vegetable Chili

3 tbsp olive oil
2 onions, chopped
2 tsp fine sugar
9oz mushrooms, sliced
2 garlic cloves, sliced
2 tsp mild chili powder
1 tbsp ground coriander
10–12oz jar sweet red pepper sauce
1 cup vegetable stock
15oz can chickpeas, drained
and rinsed
15oz can blackeyed beans, drained
and rinsed
salt & pepper to taste
rice or crusty bread, to serve

Takes 55 minutes • Serves 4

1  Heat the oil in a large, heavy-bottom saucepan.
Cook the onions and sugar over a high heat, until
deep golden. Add the mushrooms, garlic, chili
powder and ground coriander and cook for 2–3
minutes.
2  Stir in the pepper sauce, stock, chickpeas and
beans and bring to a boil.
3  Reduce the heat, cover and simmer gently for 20
minutes. Add a little extra stock if the mixture is too
thick. Season with salt and pepper and serve with
rice or crusty bread.

• Per serving: 303 calories, protein 14g, carbohydrate 36g, fat
13g, saturated fat 2g, fiber 8g, added sugar 5g, salt 1.4g

This recipe is easily multiplied to feed a crowd.
The bean mixture can be made in advance and reheated.

# Flageolet Bean Casserole

1 tbsp olive oil
3 medium zucchini,
cut into chunks
½ cup dry white wine
2½ cups of your favorite tomato
sauce
5oz pitted black olives
2 × 15oz cans flageolet or navy
beans, drained and rinsed
2 tbsp chopped fresh rosemary
salt & pepper to taste
2oz vegan margarine
2 garlic cloves, crushed
2 tbsp chopped fresh flatleaf parsley
1 medium baguette, thickly sliced

Takes 40 minutes • Serves 4

1  Heat the oil in a large frying pan, add the
zucchini and saute over a medium-high heat for 10
minutes, until softened and lightly charred.
2  Add the wine and boil rapidly for 2 minutes, until
reduced by half. Add the tomato sauce, olives, beans
and rosemary. Bring to a boil and simmer for 5
minutes. Season with salt and pepper.
3  Preheat the broiler. Combine the margarine, garlic
and parsley. Spread thickly on the bread. Arrange
the slices on a pan and broil for 5–10 minutes, until
golden.

• Per serving: 546 calories, protein 24g, carbohydrate 61g, fat
22g, saturated fat 8g, fiber 15g, added sugar none, salt 4.35g

A syllabub is a milk punch or pudding.
You can use whatever fruits are in season.

# Passion Fruit Syllabub

3 tbsp white wine
1 tbsp fine sugar
finely grated zest and juice of
1 small lemon
50z whipping cream
1 passion fruit, cut in half
starfruit slices, to decorate
vanilla wafers, to serve (optional)

Takes 10 minutes, plus marinating • Serves 2

1  Mix together the white wine, sugar and lemon zest and juice and leave for at least 30 minutes to marinate.
2  Pour the cream into the white wine mixture and, using an electric mixture, whip to soft peaks.
3  Scoop out the passion fruit flesh and seeds and stir lightly through the cream mixture. Spoon into two glasses or tumblers and decorate with the starfruit slices. Serve with dessert cookies, if you like.

• Per serving: 394 calories, protein 2.5g, carbohydrate 12g, fat 36g, saturated fat 22.5g, fiber 1g, added sugar 8g, salt 0.9g

This light, frothy mousse is best
made with a high-quality dark chocolate.

# Cappuccino Mousse

4½oz dark chocolate
1 tbsp instant coffee granules
2 tbsp Tia Maria or Kahlua (coffee
liqueur)
4 medium egg whites
5oz fine sugar
1 cup whipping cream
cocoa powder, to dust

Takes 15 minutes, plus chilling • Serves 6

1  Melt the chocolate in a bowl set over a pan of
simmering water, making sure the bowl doesn't
touch the water. Remove from the heat and cool.
Dissolve the coffee in 2 tablespoons of boiling water
and stir in the Tia Maria. Stir into the chocolate.
2  In a bowl, whisk the egg whites to soft peaks.
Gradually whisk in the fine sugar until thick. Stir 2
tablespoonfuls of the eggwhites into the chocolate
mixture, then  gently fold in the remainder. Spoon
the mousse into six cappuccino cups and chill for at
least 20 minutes.
3  Lightly whip the cream and spoon over the
mousses. Dust with cocoa, to serve.

• Per serving: 461 calories, protein 5g, carbohydrate 42g, fat
31g, saturated fat 19g, fiber 0.5g, added sugar 38g, salt 0.22g

Some supermarkets sell pineapple already
peeled and sliced, which will help to speed up this recipe.

# Pineapple with Rum and Raisins

1 ripe pineapple, peeled
1oz butter
2oz light brown sugar
1oz raisins
1oz pecans
2fl oz rum
vanilla ice cream, to serve (optional)

Takes 20 minutes • Serves 4

1 Remove the "eyes" from the pineapple. Cut in half, lengthwise, remove the center core and slice into wedges. Melt the butter in a griddle pan. Add the wedges of pineapple and cook until golden, about 3 minutes on each side.

2 Sprinkle with the sugar, raisins and pecans and cook until the sugar has melted and becomes syrupy.

3 Carefully add the rum and ignite it, using a long match. Allow the flames to die down. Serve the pineapple wedges with the sauce spooned over and a spoonful of vanilla ice cream, if you like.

• Per serving: 286 calories, protein 2g, carbohydrate 43g, fat 10g, saturated fat 3g, fiber 3g, added sugar 13g, salt 0.14g

Cut the richness of the mascarpone—a sweet
Italian cream cheese —by combining it with yogurt.

# Mascarpone Cream with Grapes

½ cup red wine
2oz fine sugar
2 tsp arrowroot
12oz seedless red or white grapes
9oz mascarpone cheese
8oz plain, mild-style yogurt
2 tbsp honey

Takes 20 minutes, plus chilling • Serves 4

1  Place the red wine and sugar in a large pan, bring to a boil and simmer until the sugar has dissolved. Mix the arrowroot with a little cold water to form a smooth paste, then stir into the wine. Boil, stirring continuously, for 1 minute, until thickened.
2  Stir the grapes into the wine mixture, bring to a boil, cover and simmer for 2 minutes. Leave to cool. Spoon into four tall glasses.
3  Put the mascarpone, yogurt and honey into a large bowl and whisk until smooth. Spoon over the grapes and chill until ready to serve.

• Per serving: 487 calories, protein 0g, carbohydrate 35g, fat 34g, saturated fat 22g, fiber 1g, added sugar 19g, salt 0.58g

A creamy yogurt ice with far fewer calories than regular ice cream. You'll find dried cranberries in larger supermarkets.

## Cranberry Yogurt Ice

4oz dried cranberries
finely grated zest and juice
of 1 orange
18fl oz mild, plain yogurt
2oz fine sugar
½ cup heavy cream
3 tbsp brandy

Takes 35 minutes • Serves 6

1  Put the cranberries, orange zest and juice and ½ cup water in a pot, bring to a boil, cover and simmer for 25 minutes, until the cranberries are very soft. Let cool completely.

2  Beat together the yogurt, sugar and cream until the sugar has partially dissolved. Stir in the brandy and pour into a freezerproof container. Freeze for 3 hours, until thickened. Stir in the cranberry mixture until well distributed.

3  Freeze until solid. Transfer to the refrigerator for about 20 minutes before serving. Use within 2 months.

• Per serving: 263 calories, protein 6g, carbohydrate 12g, fat 20g, saturated fat 12g, fiber 1g, added sugar 9g, salt 0.18g

A light raspberry and orange mixture is layered with
crunchy oat clusters to make a delightful dessert.

# Raspberry Crunch Fool

10oz raspberries,
plus extra for decorating
5oz confectioner's sugar
8oz cream cheese
14fl oz yogurt
zest and juice of 1 orange
5oz any oat cluster cereal
mint sprigs, to decorate

Takes 15 minutes, plus chilling • Serves 4

1  Put one-third of the raspberries in a food
processor with half the confectioner's sugar and
process until smooth. Strain through a sieve to
remove the pips.
2  Beat the cream cheese, yogurt, orange zest and
juice in a bowl with the remaining confectioner's
sugar, until smooth. Mix in the raspberry purée and
fold in the remaining whole raspberries.
3  Divide half the mixture among four glasses.
Sprinkle with half the cereal and spoon over another
layer of the raspberry mixture. Sprinkle on the
remaining cereal and decorate with sugar-dipped
raspberries and sprigs of mint. Chill for 1 hour
before serving.

• Per serving: 565 calories, protein 20g, carbohydrate 76g, fat
22g, saturated fat 1g, fiber 2g, added sugar 44g, salt 1.46g

You'll find dairy-free yogurt and cream cheese
in large supermarkets or health food stores.

# Peach Melba Brûlée

8oz raspberries
5oz confectioner's sugar
1 cup dairy-free yogurt
8oz dairy-free cream cheese
zest of 1 lemon
2 peaches, peeled, halved
and sliced
2oz raw sugar

Takes 25 minutes • Serves 4

1  Process half the raspberries in a food processor
with 1oz of the confectioner's sugar until smooth.
Place the remaining confectioner's sugar, dairy-free
yogurt, dairy-free cream cheese and lemon zest in a
bowl and beat well together.
2  Preheat the broiler. Divide the remaining
raspberries and the peach slices between four
ramekin dishes. Spoon on the raspberry purée.
3  Top with the yogurt mixture and sprinkle with raw
sugar. Broil until the sugar has caramelized. Cool
slightly before serving.

• Per serving: 461 calories, protein 15g, carbohydrate 62g, fat
19g, saturated fat none, fiber 2g, added sugar 52.5g, salt
0.87g

A simple dessert with
the luxurious flavor of saffron.

# Saffron Rice Pudding

large pinch of saffron strands
6oz short-grain rice
2 cups milk
1 cup heavy cream
4½oz fine sugar
finely shredded zest and juice
of 2 lemons
lemon curd and cookies,
to serve (optional)

Takes 35 minutes • Serves 4

1  Sprinkle the saffron over 2 tablespoons of hot water and leave to soak for 5 minutes.
2  Meanwhile, put the rice, milk, cream, fine sugar and half the lemon zest into a large pot. Bring to a boil, then simmer gently for 20–25 minutes, until the rice is tender and the mixture has thickened. Stir in the saffron-infused water and lemon juice.
3  Spoon into serving bowls and sprinkle with the remaining shredded lemon zest. Serve with a spoonful of lemon curd and cookies, if you like.

• Per serving: 723 calories, protein 9g, carbohydrate 81g, fat 42g, saturated fat 26g, fiber 0.02g, added sugar 33g, salt 0.29g

Raid the fruit bowl and pantry
to make this satisfying dessert.

# Tropical Fruit Crunch

2oz butter
4oz rolled oats
6 tbsp raw sugar
4 tbsp shredded coconut
2 bananas, cut into chunks
2 ripe mangoes, peeled and
cut into chunks
8oz can pineapple chunks in
natural juice, drained
custard or cream, to serve

Takes 15 minutes • Serves 4

1  Melt two-thirds of the butter in a large frying pan. Add the oats, 4 tablespoons of the raw sugar and the coconut and cook for 3–4 minutes, stirring occasionally, until crisp and golden.
2  Meanwhile, melt the remaining butter in another frying pan and add the bananas, mangoes and pineapple chunks. Sprinkle with the remaining raw sugar and cook over a low heat for 5 minutes, until the fruit is softened and caramelized.
3  Divide the fruit among four plates and sprinkle with the crunchy oat mixture. Serve with fresh custard or cream.

• Per serving: 589 calories, protein 7g, carbohydrate 91g, fat 25g, saturated fat 16g, fiber 11g, added sugar 16g, salt 0.41g

This dessert looks spectacular, but made with just four ingredients, it has got to be one of the easiest to make.

# Almond Nectarine Tart

5oz white marzipan, cut into chunks
5 tbsp heavy cream
13oz puff pastry, thawed if frozen
4 nectarines, halved, pitted and thinly sliced
crème fraîche (or heavy cream mixed with 1/2 tsp buttermilk), to serve

Takes 30 minutes • Serves 8

1 Preheat the oven to 400°F. Place the marzipan in a food processor with the cream and process to a thick paste. Roll the pastry out to a rectangle about 12 × 9-inches.

2 Lay the pastry on a baking sheet and score a line ¼-inch inside the edge all around. Spread the marzipan paste over the pastry inside the line and arrange the nectarine slices in rows on top.

3 Bake in the oven for 15–20 minutes, until the pastry is golden and risen. Cut into squares and serve with chilled crème fraîche.

• Per serving: 311 calories, protein 4g, carbohydrate 34g, fat 18g, saturated fat 7g, fiber 1g, added sugar 9g, salt 0.39g

The addition of blackberry brandy to the gooseberry filling gives the crumble an extra zing.

# Gooseberry Crumble

1lb 4oz gooseberries, tops and tails removed
6oz fine sugar
3 tbsp blackberry brandy
2½oz butter, diced, at room temperature, plus extra for greasing
6oz all-purpose flour
2oz pecan, roughly chopped
fresh custard, ice cream or cream, to serve

Takes 55 minutes • Serves 6

1  Preheat the oven to 375°F. Grease a 1-quart baking dish. Put the gooseberries, two-thirds of the sugar and the cassis in a pot and cook gently for 5 minutes, until the fruit is soft. Transfer to the greased dish.
2  To make the crumble, rub the butter into the flour until the mixture resembles rough breadcrumbs. Stir in the remaining sugar and pecans. Add the gooseberries and level the surface. Bake for 30–40 minutes, until the topping is golden.
3  Divide the crumble among individual serving bowls and serve immediately with fresh custard, ice cream or pouring cream.

• Per serving: 381 calories, protein 5g, carbohydrate 57g, fat 17g, saturated fat 7g, fiber 4g, added sugar 31g, salt 0.25g

A lovely autumn pudding that's easily adapted to use most fruits in season. Serve with heavy cream.

# Apple and Blackberry Pudding

2½oz self-rising flour
2½oz vegetable shortening
4oz white breadcrumbs
finely grated zest and juice of
1 large orange
5 tbsp milk
1oz butter
1 large eating apple, peeled, cored
and roughly chopped
4oz blackberries
4oz fine sugar
heavy cream, to serve

Takes 55 minutes • Serves 6

1 Preheat the oven to 400°F. Sift the flour into a bowl, stir in a pinch of salt, the shortening, breadcrumbs, orange zest and just enough milk to make a soft crumble mix.
2 Melt the butter in a large frying pan and cook the apple for 5 minutes, until softened. Stir into the crumble mix, then spread into a 1-quart dish. Sprinkle the blackberries on top.
3 Put the orange juice, sugar and ½ cup water in a pan. Heat, stirring, until dissolved, then boil rapidly until pale golden. Pour over the pudding. Leave to soak for 10 minutes, then bake for 25 minutes. Serve hot or warm with heavy cream.

• Per serving: 286 calories, protein 5g, carbohydrate 56g, fat 6g, saturated fat 3g, fiber 2g, added sugar 22g, salt 0.57g

# Index

almonds
    and nectarine tart 206–7
    with stir-fried salad 50–1
apples
    and blackberry pudding
        210–11
    and pumpkin curry 128–9
avocado omelette, soufflé 60–1

bagels with vegetables 168–9
beans
    chili bean open lasagne 98–9
    flageolet casserole 186–7
    flageolet and feta salad 32–3
    flageolet with pasta 88–9
    and vegetable chili 184–5
    fava with gnocchi 106–7
    fava minty paté 166–7
    white bean and celery salad
        20–1
beets
    roasted with horseradish
        124–5
    and tzatziki sandwich 36–7
blackberry and apple pudding
    210–11
blinis, vegetable stacks 52–3

bread pudding, cheesy 82–3
broccoli
    and poached egg toasts 44–5
    and walnut spaghetti 172–3
bruschettas, stuffed mushroom
    68–9

cabbage, red salad, warm 160–1
cannelloni, cheese and tomato
    100–1
capers 60
cappuccino mousse 190–1
casserole, flageolet bean 186–7
cauliflower pasta, spicy 92–3
celeriac and blue cheese soup
    12–13
celery
    and orange salad 158–9
    and white bean salad 20–1
chapati wraps, spicy vegetable
    56–7
cheese 24, 52, 68
    blue cheese and celeriac soup
        12–13
    blue cheese and vegetable
        gratin 144–5
    bread pudding 82–3

brie and tomato tart 66–7
cheddar and tomato rice
    112–13
and chutney melts 70–1
feta and flageolet salad 32–3
feta and charred peach
    salad 28–9
feta, red onion and olive tart
    150–1
goat's cheese with eggplant
    136–7
goat's cheese and leek tarts
    148–9
goat's cheese salad 30–1
goat's cheese and tomato
    crumble 140–1
mascarpone cream with
    grapes 194–5
paneer and pea curry 138–9
polenta dolcelatte grill 78–9
ricotta and olive paté 46–7
ricotta-stuffed crispbreads 42–3
scallion tart 152–3
smoked cheese and tomato
    pita 40–1
smoked cheese and vegetable
    fry 76–7

stilton and walnut tart 84–5
taleggio with pasta 94–5
and tomato cannelloni 100–1
two cheese salad with croutons 24–5
chickpea salad, Indian 132–3
chili 92, 96
bean open lasagne 98–9
bean and vegetable 184–5
chive and tomato tart 64–5
chutney and cheese melts 70–1
coconut
spicy vegetables 182–3
Thai vegetable soup 54–5
conversion tables 8–9
couscous
roasted vegetable 134–5
tofu and pepper 80–1
cranberry yogurt ice 196–7
crispbreads, ricotta-stuffed 42–3
croutons with two cheese salad 24–5
crumble
gooseberry 208–9
tomato and goat's cheese 140–1
crunch, tropical fruit 204–5
cucumber 36
curry
creamy egg 154–5
paste, Thai 54
pea and paneer 138–9
pumpkin and apple 128–9
eggs 90

creamy curry 154–5
egg and broccoli toasts 44–5
with rösti and onions 58–9
eggplant
with goat's cheese 136–7
with pasta 176–7
English garden salad 26–7

fennel and cracked wheat salad 164–5
Fiorentina baked pasta 102–3
focaccia, stuffed 170–1
fool, raspberry crunch 198–9

Genovese spaghetti 86–7
gnocchi
with fava beans 106–7
lemon butter 104–5
gooseberry crumble 208–9
grapes with mascarpone cream 194–5
gratin, blue cheese vegetable 144–5
Greek pasta salad 34–5

herb stuffed mushrooms 72–3
horseradish with roasted beets 124–5

ice, cranberry yogurt 196–7
Indian chickpea salad 132–3

kumquat and mushroom salad, hot 22–3

lasagne, chili bean open 98–9
leeks
and goat's cheese tarts 148–9
and mushroom risotto 108–9
and saffron soup 18–19
lemon 92, 96
butter with gnocchi 104–5
lemongrass 16

mint 26
fava bean minty paté 166–7
spring vegetables 48–9
mousse, cappuccino 190–1
muffin, mini, pizzas 38–9
mushrooms 112
herb stuffed 72–3
and kumquat salad, hot 22–3
and leek risotto 108–9
stuffed bruschettas 68–9

nasi goreng, spicy 116–17
nectarine and almond tart 206–7
noodles
crispy salad, warm 180–1
and sesame salad 118–19
Thai satay 122–3
Tom Yam 178–9
and watercress salad 162–3

olives 34, 60
and red onion and feta tart 150–1
and ricotta paté 46–7
omelette, avocado soufflé 60–1

onions 22
  and potato tart 130–1
  red onion with feta and olive
    tart 150–1
  with rösti and egg 58–9
  scallion cheese tart
    152–3
  and celery salad 158–9

passion fruit syllabub 188–9
pasta
  with eggplant 176–7
  Fiorentina baked 102–3
  with flageolet beans 88–9
  Greek pasta salad 34–5
  ravioli with pumpkin 96–7
  spaghetti carbonara 90–1
  spaghetti Genovese 86–7
  spicy cauliflower 92–3
  with spicy peas 174–5
  with taleggio 94–5
  walnut and broccoli spaghetti
    172–3
paté
  minty fava bean 166–7
  olive and ricotta 46–7
peach
  charred with feta salad 28–9
  Melba brûlée 200–1
peas 112
  and paneer curry 138–9
  spicy peas with pasta 174–5
pepper and tofu couscous
  80–1

pine nuts 92
pineapple with rum and raisins
  192–3
pita, smoked cheese and
  tomato 40–1
pizzas
  mini muffin 38–9
  polenta 142–3
polenta
  dolcelatte grill 78–9
  pizza 142–3
  pizza-topped 74–5
  spring vegetable 126–7
potatoes
  and onion tart 130–1
  rösti with egg and onions 58–9
  spinach and sage soup 10–11
puddings
  apple and blackberry 210–11
  cheesy bread 82–3
  saffron rice 202–3
pumpkin
  and apple curry 128–9
  with ravioli 96–7
quark 126
quiche, crustless vegetable 62–3

raisins and rum with pineapple
  192–3
raspberry crunch fool 198–9
ravioli with pumpkin 96–7
rice
  and baby spinach soup 14–15
  cheddar and tomato 112–13

saffron rice pudding 202–3
  spicy nasi goreng 116–17
  Thai fried with vegetables
    114–15
risotto
  baked spinach 110–11
  leek and mushroom 108–9
rocket 52
rösti with egg and onions 58–9
rum and raisins with pineapple
  192–3

saffron
  and leek soup 18–19
  rice pudding 202–3
sage 96
  spinach and potato soup
    10–11
salads
  celery and white bean 20–1
  cracked wheat and fennel
    164–5
  crispy noodle, warm 180–1
  English garden 26–7
  feta and charred peach 28–9
  goat's cheese 30–1
  Greek pasta 34–5
  Indian chickpea 132–3
  mushroom and kumquat 22–3
  noodle and watercress 162–3
  orange and celery 158–9
  red cabbage, warm 160–1
  sesame noodle 118–19
  stir-fried with almonds 50–1

Tuscan 156–7
two cheese with croutons 24–5
sandwich
    beet and tzatziki 36–7
    ricotta-stuffed crispbreads 42–3
sesame noodle salad 118–19
soups
    baby spinach and rice 14–15
    celeriac and blue cheese
        12–13
    corn, hot and sour 16–17
    saffron and leek 18–19
    spinach, sage and potato
        10–11
    Thai coconut vegetable 54–5
spaghetti
    carbonara 90–1
    Genovese 86–7
    walnut and broccoli 172–3
spinach
    baked risotto 110–11
    and rice soup 14–15
    and sage and potato soup
        10–11
syllabub, passion fruit 188–9

tapenade 60
tarts
    almond and nectarine 206–7
    brie and tomato 66–7
    cheesy spring onion 152–3
    leek and goat's cheese 148–9
    potato and onion 130–1
    red onion, feta and olive 150–1

stilton and walnut 84–5
tomato and chive 64–5
toasts, broccoli and egg 44–5
tofu
    chow mein 120–1
    tofu and pepper couscous
        80–1
Tom Yam noodles 178–9
tomatoes 20, 34, 52
    and brie tart 66–7
    and cheddar rice 112–13
    and cheese cannelloni 100–1
    and chive tart 64–5
    and goat's cheese crumble
        140–1
    and smoked cheese pita 40–1
tropical fruit crunch 204–5
Tuscan salad 156–7
tzatziki and beet sandwich
    36–7

vegetables
    and bean chili 184–5
    blini stacks 52–3
    crustless vegetable quiche
        62–3
    gratin with blue cheese 144–5
    griddled with bagels 168–9
    roasted vegetable couscous
        134–5
    root vegetable bake 146–7
    smoked cheese vegtable fry
        76–7
    spicy chapati wraps 56–7

spicy coconut 182–3
spring, minted 48–9
spring vegetable polenta
    126–7
Thai coconut soup 54–5

walnut
    and broccoli spaghetti 172–3
    and stilton tart 84–5
watercress and noodle salad
    162–3
wheat, cracked and fennel salad
    164–5
wine, white 20

yogurt
    cranberry ice 196–7
    tzatziki and beet sandwich
        36–7

# Photo credits and recipe credits

BBC Worldwide would like to thank the following for providing photographs. While every effort has been made to trace and acknowledge all photographers, we would like to apologize if there are any errors or omissions.

Chris Alack p21, p105, p159, p171, p179, p205; Marie-Louise Avery p65, p101; Iain Bagwell p87; Clive Bozzard-Hill p31, p59, p161, p203; Peter Cassidy p49, p125, p207, p211; Ken Field p13, p19, p47, p109, p117, p123, p129; Dave King p111, p139, p191; Richard Kolker p23, p37, p121; David Munns p25; Myles New p57; Thomas Odulate p39, p153, p195, p199, p201; William Reavell p11, p41, p107, p127, p133, p137, p151, p165, p181, p193, p197; Howard Shooter p15, p29, p163; Simon Smith p81, p97, p115, p155; Roger Stowell p27, p33, p35, p75, p77, p113, p145, p147; Sam Stowell p45, p157, p167, p209; Mark Thompson p131; Trevor Vaughan p53, 61, p71, p79, p99, p103, p135, p143, p149, p187, p189; Ian Wallace p43, p175; Simon Wheeler p67, p69, p85, p141, p185; Jonathan Whitaker p17, p55, p119; Frank Wieder p63, p73, p83, p89, p91, p93, p95, p177, p183; BBC Worldwide p51, p169, p173

All the recipes in this book have been created by the editorial teams on *BBC Good Food Magazine* and *BBC Vegetarian Good Food Magazine*.

Angela Boggiano, Lorna Brash, Sara Buenfeld, Mary Cadogan, Gilly Cubitt, Barney Desmazery, Joanna Farrow, Rebecca Ford, Silvana Franco, Catherine Hill, Jane Lawrie, Clare Lewis, Sara Lewis, Liz Martin, Kate Moseley, Orlando Murrin, Vicky Musselman, Angela Nilsen, Justine Pattison, Jenny White and Jeni Wright.